The Fourth
# Frank Muir
# Goes Into...

# The Fourth
# Frank Muir
# Goes Into...

FRANK MUIR

and

SIMON BRETT

 Robson Books

FIRST PUBLISHED IN GREAT BRITAIN IN 1981 BY ROBSON BOOKS LTD, BOLSOVER HOUSE, 5–6 CLIPSTONE STREET, LONDON W1P 7EB. COPYRIGHT © 1981 FRANK MUIR AND SIMON BRETT.

Permission to use extracts from the following copyright material is gratefully acknowledged:

*This England* by Michael Bateman (Statesman & Nation Publishing Co); *Funny Ha Ha and Funny Peculiar* and *Funny Ha Ha and Funny Hilarious* by Denys Parsons (Pan Books); *The Best of Beachcomber* edited by Richard Ingrams (Frederick Muller Ltd); *Cautionary Verses* by Hilaire Belloc (Gerald Duckworth & Co); *It Must Be True* by Denys Parsons (Macdonald); *Salome Dear, Not in the Fridge* selected by Arthur Marshall (Allen & Unwin); *You Have Been Warned* by W. D. H. McCullough (Methuen & Co); quotation from Ogden Nash (The Estate of Ogden Nash); *The Times* letter, the Very Reverend Hugh White-Thomson.

Picture Sources: Barnaby's Picture Library, The Fotomas Library, Punch. and grateful thanks to the London Library.

Designed by Harold King.

Muir, Frank
    The fourth Frank Muir goes into —
    1. English wit and humor
    I. Title   II. Brett, Simon, *1945-*
    828'.91407   PN6175

    ISBN 0-86051-147-2

Printed in Hungary.

# CONTENTS

# MONEY

A Scot goes into a Jewish tailor's shop and asks to see the best suit in the shop. The proprietor shows him one. 'Look at this, sir,' he says 'and it's not £100! Not even £50 – £40 and it's yours.'

The Scot felt the cloth. 'I wouldn't give you £30 for it – not even £25! £20 is my price.'

'Right you are, it's yours,' said the proprietor. 'That's the way I like to do business – no haggling.'


Doctor, doctor, I've come to see you about my little boy who was brought into hospital yesterday after swallowing 50p.

Oh yes.

How is he?

No change yet.


Four thugs tried to mug an Irishman, but he put up a tremendous fight and it took them half an hour to overpower him. When they did, they found he only had 3p in his pocket.

'Why on earth did you put up such a fight for 3p?' asked one of the thugs.

'Sure,' said the Irishman, 'I thought you were after the ten pound note in me sock.'


Did you hear about the Scotsman who died and left his cousin all the money that his cousin owed him?


A man paid £500 for a talking dog and took it into the pub to show it off. No one would believe him and they offered him 10 to 1 that the dog couldn't talk.

'I'll show you,' he said and ordered the dog to speak. Nothing, not a word. All the people in the pub roared their heads off.

'You've been done,' they cried as they left.

When they'd gone, the man turned to the dog in disgust. 'Why wouldn't you talk, you stupid animal?'

The dog winked. 'Not so much of the stupid. Next week we'll get odds of 100 to 1 and we'll both clean up.'

Have you heard about this deep-freeze reanimation? Simple, really. The idea is that you get yourself deep frozen while you're still alive and then get thawed out after twenty years or so – when the economic climate's better. Get the idea? I mean, if Louis XIV did it, he'd be a Bourbon on the rocks. Well, there was a bloke who had this done – invested all his money – £10,000 – in stocks and shares and got himself deep frozen. Twenty years later he was thawed out and his first action was to leap into a phone-box and ring his stockbroker.

'Tell me,' he asked, 'how much is my £10,000 worth now?'

'It's worth two and a quarter billion pounds,' said the stockbroker.

'Good gracious,' cried the man, 'that's amazing.'

But then he was interrupted by the operator's voice saying, 'Your time is up. Will you put in two billion pounds for the next two minutes?'

I wish I had the money to buy an elephant.

Why on earth do you want an elephant?

I don't. I just wish I had the money.

What is it, doctor?

I have decided to double my fee in your case, as of today.

But why, doctor? I'm not a bit better, and I've been coming to see you for four years now –

That's why.

Hymie was discussing business with a friend.

'A lady walked into the shop – wanted a fur coat. I said, here, I've got a lovely mink – a great bargain. It cost me a thousand pounds, it's worth fifteen hundred, you can have it for £750 – I made a pound.'

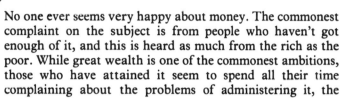

No one ever seems very happy about money. The commonest complaint on the subject is from people who haven't got enough of it, and this is heard as much from the rich as the poor. While great wealth is one of the commonest ambitions, those who have attained it seem to spend all their time complaining about the problems of administering it, the amount they are taxed on it and how little satisfaction it brings.

But, satisfactory or not, money is essential. And always has been. The poet Horace:

> **By honest means, if you can, but by any means make money.**

Samuel Butler:

> **It has been said that the love of money is the root of all evil. The want of money is so quite as truly.**

Yes, you've got to have money. And once you've got it, to keep it. Sholom Aleichem:

> **Money is round. It rolls away.**

It certainly does. How do people manage to live within their incomes? Domestic economies help, but some people take that sort of thing to extremes. An extract from a letter to *The Times:*

> **I, too, can remember buying matches at 1¼d. a dozen boxes; now that they are 2d. a box, I split each of its 40 contents into two with an old safety razor blade (it is easily done) and so get 80 for my 2d.**

Really, the only way to manage money is to know at all times how much you can spend. In the words of Josh Billings:

**Live within your income, even if you have to borrow money to do so.**

Borrowing money is not always easy, though. There seems a marked reluctance on the part of banks to shell out to really deserving causes. An anonymous thought on the subject:

**A banker is a fellow who will lend you money if you can prove that you don't need it.**

*"If God had meant us to live within our means He wouldn't have given us credit cards!"*

And another from Robert Frost:

**A bank is a place where they lend you an umbrella in fair weather and ask for it back again when it begins to rain.**

Bankers have always got good reasons why they can't lend you money and there is one common factor in all these reasons – it's never the bank's fault. It's due to fluctuations on the world markets or the run on the pound or, more likely, government policy. There's always a freeze on somewhere and whoever's Chancellor is always doing something to make things difficult for you. The next quotation comes from a *News Chronicle* report of 1952, but really it's timeless:

> **The Chancellor seemed to rule out in advance any hopeful and constructive action – except more import cuts. No reduction in wages, no reduction in the standard of living, no unemployment, no economies . . . nothing.**

When there is government control on incomes, it affects everyone. Well, nearly everyone. A report from the *Sunday Express*:

> **A spokesman at Buckingham Palace denied that the Prince would be beating the incomes freeze. 'It is not that sort of income,' he said. 'It simply means that he will get a larger share of the revenue from his estates than he did previously.'**

If you don't happen to be a prince, and you can't borrow any money, then the best thing you can do is to increase your existing stock by judicious investment. This makes good sense, according to the advice given by his father to Texas financier Clint Murchison Jnr:

> **Money is like manure. If you spread it around, it does a lot of good. But if you pile it up in one place, it stinks like hell.**

Investment is a risky business and perhaps it's best to go for something comparatively safe. Oliver Wendell Holmes:

> **Put not your trust in money, but put your money in trust.**

Or maybe minimize your risks even further. Kin Hubbard:

> **The safest way to double your money is to fold it over once and put it in your pocket.**

But if you do set out on the hazardous trail of investment, bear in mind the advice of Billy Rose:

**Never invest your money in anything that eats or needs repainting.**

*"I like it, Pickering. You've caught me at the peak of the market."*

Forearmed with that, you would not fall for a seductive proposition like this one advertised in *World's Fair:*

**For hire for the season. Seaside or tour. Shares only. The World's Ugliest Woman. Weight 18 stone. 31 years old. One tooth. Face full of wrinkles like a prune. Charming personality.**

But say your investments are successful, say you make a great deal of money . . . does it help? What's the use of making an enormous amount, when the tax man waits round the next corner to mug you and take everything away? Tax is a serious problem – a letter to the *People*:

> **For years I have claimed Income Tax allowance as a married man, although I am single. I now wish to marry but am afraid to do so in case the tax men find out. What is your advice?**

Many people seem to be on the fiddle these days. In fact, they always have been, in spite of what Dr. Johnson once wrote:

> **There are few ways in which a man can be more innocently employed than in getting money.**

A great many ways of getting money are, I'm afraid, far from innocent. Dubious practice occurs at the highest level of business. Let's hear a little courtroom exchange from the old *News Chronicle*:

> **'It's a lie, isn't it?'**
> **'It's not exactly a lie, sir, it is a commercial term.'**

And that's only the beginning. Another commercial term which often crops up in discussions of money matters is 'stealing'. And it starts among the youngest members of society. A report from the *Gloucestershire Echo*:

> **After a school lesson demonstrating the value of money, a nine-year-old girl stole £1.12s. of the cash used in the demonstration.**

Or another from the *Daily Telegraph*:

> **Three Sidcup boys admitted at Tower Bridge Juvenile Court, London, stealing 7s. 1d. from a car. When sharing the money, they threw 1s. 1d. away to make division easier, a detective said.**

But nowadays delinquent children may find it hard to keep their ill-gotten gains safe from other members of their households. Here is the testimony of a wife in a North Kent Court, quoted in the *Evening News:*

> **My husband cut himself so severely in forcing open the children's money-box that he had to spend the contents on lint and bandages.**

The trouble is that criminals are getting increasingly familiar in their approaches. Let's hear a report from the *Daily Express*:

> **When Mrs Janet Trent opened her diary yesterday the entry for the day was already filled in by someone else and read: 'House burgled 5 a.m.' A burglar had stolen £24 as she slept in her Hallfield Estate, Paddington, home.**

Which prompts a little quotation from Samuel Butler:

> **Brigands demand your money or your life; women require both.**

But the fact remains that money is powerful and the wealthy can often dictate their own terms. T. E. Brown on the subject:

> **Money is honey, my little sonny,**
> **And a rich man's joke is always funny.**

Fred Allen:

> **Money talks – and it is the only conversation worth hearing when times are bad.**

E. W. Howe was not so convinced:

> **When a man says money can do anything, that settles it; he hasn't any.**

And if you want a little sour grapes comfort, try this anonymous New England saying:

> **If you want to know what God thinks of money, look at the people he gives it to.**

And, continuing this reassurance therapy for the deprived, here are the views of a man who's been there, a man who's had it all and is therefore in a position to pontificate on money. The American multi-millionaire, Joseph Hirshhorn:

> **After the first million, it doesn't matter. You can only eat three meals a day – I tried eating four and I got sick. You can't sleep in more than one bed a night. Maybe I have twenty suits, but I can only wear one at a time, and I can't use more than two shirts a day.**

And that's about it for money. Just a couple of thoughts before the end of the chapter. First, a sensational headline from the *Chicago Daily News:*

> **Seven million dollar expansion cost seven million million dollars.**

And, finally, a definition quoted in a Glasgow newspaper early in this century:

> **A tip is a small sum of money you give to somebody because you're afraid he won't like not being paid for something you haven't asked him to do.**

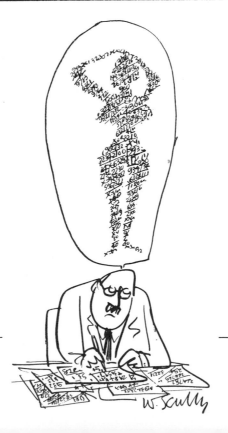

W. Scully

# PUBLIC TRANSPORT

An Irishman went to visit his friend in hospital. There was the friend spreadeagled on the bed, suspended from pulleys, every limb in plaster, bandaged up like the invisible man.

'Oh, you look terrible, Paddy. What happened?'

'Well, Mick, I was working on the railway line down in a cutting, and a train came along. I ran like mad alone the line, but it was too fast for me.'

'But Paddy, why did you run along the line, why didn't you run up the embankment?'

'Now, Mick, if it beat me on the flat, what chance would I have had uphill?'

STATION ANNOUNCEMENT: The train now arriving at platforms 16, 17, 18, 19 and 20 is coming in sideways.

There was once an Aberdonian who used to run behind the local bus every day on his way to work and gloat about the 8p he was saving.

'Why don't you run behind a taxi?' suggested his friend. 'That way you'll save 80p – and a tip.'

Did you hear about the Irish level crossing attendant who kept one gate open because he was half-expecting a train?

There was a woman on a crowded bus laden with parcels and when the conductor asked for her fare, search and fumble though she did, she couldn't reach her purse.

'It's all right,' said a man standing in front of her. 'I'll pay her fare.'

'Oh, that's very kind,' said the woman.

'Don't mention it,' he replied. 'I had to do something. You've unbuttoned my flies four times and I was getting nervous.'

Did you hear about the Scotsman who died on a Pay-as-you-Leave bus?

Once there was a bus conductor in the United States who was accused of pushing a passenger off the bus while it was in motion and killing him. He was found guilty and sentenced to the electric chair. When he was strapped in for execution, they offered him a last request and he asked for a banana. After he'd eaten the banana, it was time for him to go, and they switched on the power. Nothing. He just sat there – quite unharmed. They had another try and went through the whole process again. He ate another banana, they threw the switch – nothing. A third time – a third banana – power on – it still didn't affect him.

Well, after the third failure they were bound by law to release him and as the executioner undid the straps, he said, 'That's incredible. All those volts going through you and it has no effect. What's with the bananas?'

'Oh, it's not the bananas,' came the reply. 'It's just that I'm a bad conductor.'

I think I'd better make clear right from the start what this chapter on Public Transport is going to be about. It'll be mostly about buses and trains. I'm sorry to have to spell that out so baldly, but transport is an area where definitions sometimes get a little hazy. To prove the point, here's a quotation from the *Daily Mail*:

**The Prime Minister said it was a loose classification by the Board of Trade. 'Locomotives, ships, and aircraft' should have read 'Wire mattresses, tacks, nails, and manhole covers'.**

Let's start with the bus. And if we miss it, there'll be another one along in a minute. It's funny – that's probably the first thing one thinks of about buses – their herd instinct. You very rarely see one on its own, they tend to come in little bunches. On encountering such a bunch, you should bear in mind this advice from a Yorkshire paper:

**Although three buses might come along at the same time, passengers should be allowed to board only one at a time.**

Buses are very easy to recognize, but just in case you have difficulty spotting them, this little verse from A. D. Godley should help:

**What is it that roareth thus?**
**Can it be a Motor Bus?**
**Yes, the smell and hideous hum**
**Indicat Motorem Bum.**

People are not very kind about buses on the whole. One hears constant complaints about long waits at bus stops, about the slowness of the vehicles when they arrive, about the petty regulations for passengers.

Mind you, some of those regulations can be circumvented. An anonymous limerick:

> There was an old man of Darjeeling,
> Who boarded a bus bound for Ealing,
> He saw on the door:
> 'Please don't spit on the floor.'
> So he stood up and spat on the ceiling.

If you do get annoyed on a bus there is absolutely no point in taking it out on the machine itself. A little poem by W. J. Turner (Henry Airbubble) makes this point:

> You cannot cuss
> The motor bus
> And brilliant wit
> Is lost on it.

THOMSON'S ROAD STEAMER

What you can cuss is the conductor and poor conductors have to weather a lot of abuse from their passengers. Most of it is undeserved; it's just that people have to release their frustrations somehow. Being a bus conductor is a potentially depressing job and perhaps steps should be taken to liven it up. Here's a suggestion from *Picture Post*:

> **In Geneva, the Swiss tram conductors blow blasts on hunting horns whenever any new fare pays up. In my considered opinion, the adoption of this custom would give English conductors a greater pride in their work.**

There is a minority of bus conductors who don't seem to feel the public service element in their job as much as they should. A report from the *Daily Mirror*:

**I wondered why my bus was going so fast late at night. Then the conductor said, 'We're nipping along sharpish to miss the cinema crowds.'**

The passenger/bus conductor relationship has spawned a whole series of format jokes. I would be failing in my duty if I didn't include a few:

**Conductor, conductor, do you stop at the Dorchester Hotel?**
    **What – on my salary?**

**Conductor, conductor, are you going to Clapham?**
    **Only if they're very good, sir.**

**Conductor, conductor, are you going to Turnham Green?**
    **If I can get the paint, sir, yes.**

**Conductor, conductor, am I all right for Barking?**
    **I don't know. I haven't heard you.**

**Conductor, conductor, does this bus stop at the Embankment?**

**Well if it doesn't, sir, there's going to be one hell of a splash.**

And so on and so on *ad nauseum* and way beyond.

But let's move from the ridiculous to the sublime – to romance on a bus. A letter to *Woman's Mirror*:

**Dear Marje, I'm 15 and I often see a boy on the bus when I go home from work. I always try to sit by him because I like him very much, but he won't have anything to do with me. I work in a fish and chip shop, and can never seem to get rid of the smell. Do you think this is the trouble?**

I think that's enough of buses. Let's change to trains. The British railway system often seems confusing, particularly to outsiders. Here's the view of the American writer, Margaret Halsey:

**English trains apparently make a habit of always going toward London, and when they get there, are taken apart and mailed back to Land's End and Edinburgh.**

To understand the railways it is essential to consult the timetable. This will enable you to organize your life with as much exactness as the lady in this anonymous limerick:

There was an old lady named Carr,
Who took the three-three to Forfar,
   For she said, 'I believe
   It is likely to leave
Far before the four-four to Forfar.'

But the trouble is that timetables sometimes seem to be works of fiction, particularly when trains are delayed or cancelled due to unforeseen circumstances. The reasons for cancellation are many, though usually it's a cable fire three stations up the line – whatever that means.

Here's a report from the *Daily Worker*:

**Three trains between Dudley and Walsall, which have been cancelled to save fuel, are still running – but, to show that they are officially cancelled, no passengers are allowed to travel on them.**

Actually, to be fair on British Rail, cancellations and delays are not the major reasons why people miss trains. Often the fault is with the passengers. Some people just cannot do it. G. K. Chesterton:

**The only way to catch a train I ever discovered is to miss the train before.**

For some passengers, cutting it fine is half the fun. Here's a description of a character by Gwen Raverat:

**But she never, never missed the train. I think she felt that it would not have been sporting to start in time; it would not have given the train a fair chance of getting away without her.**

This human frailty of habitual lateness makes the running of the railways extremely difficult. It's impossible to please all of the people all of the time. Here's a report from *The Times*:

**A British Railways punctuality drive, seeking to get trains running strictly to time, has had unforeseen results for railway staffs on some main line stations. 'People have come to rely on trains being late,' said a Derby ticket collector today. 'Now many are leaving on time and we get people dashing through the barrier at the last minute and returning to complain that they've missed their train. When we explain politely that the train left on time they become abusive.'**

You can't win. Run all the trains late to satisfy that lot and you're going to start getting complaints of the other sort. From the *Daily Mail*:

> **A railway official admitted that the train had a bad record and said that he could not dispute Mr Hearsey's claim that it had been late almost every day for the past seven months. 'The only thing that we suggest is that they should allow for the train to be late as they would if it was really supposed to take longer on its journey.'**

Another popular butt of humour is British Rail food. You know, all those cruel jokes about wringing out dishcloths into the tea-cups and polystyrene cakes and how the sandwiches are put in curlers. All, I'm sure, most unjustified. Again, the customer is often at fault. News from the *Edinburgh Evening Dispatch*:

> **Miss L —— said she always asked for apple juice on train journeys because she knew it was not sold.**

The railways also suffer from dissension within their own ranks on the subject of food. Here's a report from the *Daily Express*:

> **'We run our cars like first-class hotels,' said a Pullman official rather snootily to me yesterday. 'On British Railways meals are merely for people who want to eat.'**

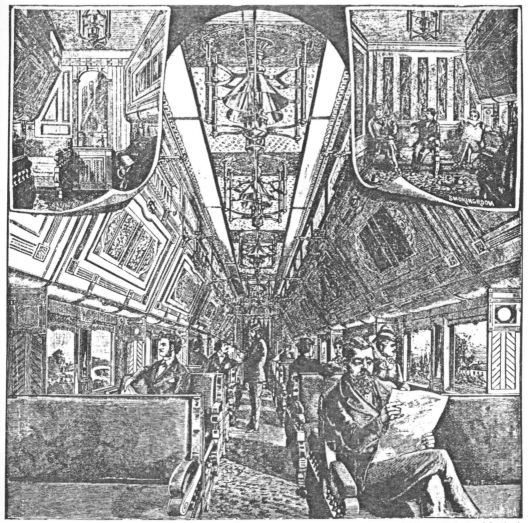

Interior View of the New Pullman Palace Sleeping Cars now Running on the Northern Pacific R. R. through between St. Paul and Portland.

And, apropos of absolutely nothing, here's an anonymous limerick:

> There was a young lady of Spain
> Who often got sick on a train,
>     Not once and again
>     But again and again
> And again and again and again.

How fortunate that there is a correct social observance for every occasion. A letter from *Picture Post*:

**People who find it necessary to vomit whilst in a railway carriage should discreetly use their hats – this would come naturally to anyone properly brought up.**

*Juvenile.* " DO YOU OBJECT TO MY SMOKING A CIGAR, SIR ? "
*Elderly Party.* " OH NO, CERTAINLY NOT, IF IT DOESN'T MAKE YOU SICK ! "

There's always someone about with a helpful suggestion. Here's another from a letter to the *Daily Mirror* on that old cause for complaint – cleanliness on the railways:

**Dandruff may be contracted by resting the head against infected upholstery in railway carriages. I suggest, therefore, that railway carriages should be boiled for twenty minutes at each station or halt.**

Actually, standards of cleanliness do occasionally slip. The *Daily Mirror* again:

A member of the platform staff admitted that the station *was* a bit grubby. 'In the past we've always waited for a strong wind to blow the dust away,' he said.

That's quite enough knocking British Rail. Let's have a go at a passenger again. How about this one reported in the *News of the World*:

When Det. Sgt. Nicholls asked, 'What's the idea?' Cathie replied: 'Everybody has his own peculiarities; this is mine.' He said he had been travelling naked in trains for about two years, but did not think anyone had seen him.

I'll close the chapter with a couple of thoughts on buses and trains. First, an anonymous epitaph:

The manner of her death was thus:
She was druv over by a bus.

And, finally, a notice from a Durham level crossing:

Beware of trains going both ways at once.

Now that motors are sweeping the children off the roads, the railway tracks remain their only available playground. At least you know where you are with a train.

# THE MOTOR CAR

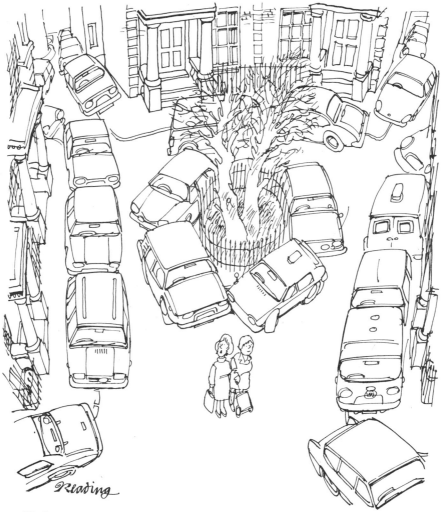

"I always think they make a nice splash of colour at this time of year."

A woman got a new car and three days later she went back to the garage where she'd bought it.

'Am I to understand,' she asked, 'that the guarantee covers anything that breaks?'

'Yes,' said the dealer.

'In that case,' she replied, 'I'd like a bicycle, a garden fence, two gateposts and a garage door.'

An Irishman was driving his lorry and suddenly turned right. When he did so, the little car behind crashed into the back of him. The car driver leapt out in fury.

'Why didn't you indicate or put your hand out?'

'Well now,' said the Irishman, 'If you couldn't see the lorry, how could you see my hand?'

Prisoner at the Bar, you are accused of driving up a one-way street.

But, your honour, I was only going one way.

Didn't you see the arrows?

Arrows? I didn't even see the Indians.

Where were you going?

I can't remember. But everyone else seemed to be coming back.

I've got some great gadgets on my car – a special carburettor that save me 50% on petrol; special spark plugs that save me 60%; and special points that save me 70%. Sometimes, if I drive too far, the petrol tank starts to overflow.

Did you hear about that terrible crash between two taxis in Aberdeen – forty-two people killed.

*The Beeston motor cab.*

A man had spent the whole evening in the pub and he was so drunk when he left that he decided the only safe way to drive home was to follow the rear lights of another car. One was just pulling out of the car park, so he started up and followed behind, guided by the lights.

All went fine for about six miles, when suddenly the lights in front went out and the drunk's car rammed into the other with a frightful crunch. The drunk leapt out of his car angrily.

'What do you think you're playing at – switching your lights off and stopping like that?'

'Why shouldn't I?' asked the other driver. 'I'm in my own garage.'

Incidentally, don't drink and drive – it slops all over the steering wheel.

There was once a vicar who had a very far-flung parish and he found that he just hadn't time to visit all his parishioners on foot. So he decided to buy a car. But vicar's salaries are small and he couldn't afford much, so he was delighted when he saw an advertisement for a car at fifteen pounds.

The address was a local farm, so he went along to have a look. The farmer showed him a terrible wreck of a machine. It was in a barn covered with straw and chicken droppings. Still, the vicar was above worldy considerations and knew that appearances did not matter. But he thought he ought to look under the bonnet and, when he did so, was distressed to find that there was no engine.

He turned reproachfully to the farmer and said, 'But how does it go?'

'Oh, don't 'ee worry about that,' said the farmer, and he called out, 'Chuckles! Chuckles!'

As he did so, an enormous chicken, about ten feet tall, appeared round the door of the barn. 'That's how it goes,' said the farmer. 'We harness up old Chuckles here and he'll pull the car anywhere you want.'

Well, the vicar thought it was a bit unconventional, but he was hard up and he did need a car, so he agreed to take it. 'How do I make it go faster?' he asked after the enormous chicken had been harnessed up.

'Oh, you just say "Faster, Chuckles, faster",' said the farmer. 'Cheerio. Good luck to 'ee.'

The vicar set off in his car at a sedate pace, but then decided that he ought to give his new car a proper test drive, so he drove out on to the M.1.

He started in the inside lane and Chuckles pulled him along at a steady thirty miles an hour. Then he thought he might be a bit daring and said, 'Faster, Chuckles, faster!' The chicken pulled out into the middle lane and speeded up. Fifty miles an hour, sixty, seventy. At that moment a huge Rolls-Royce swept past them. The vicar's competitive instinct was aroused. 'Faster, Chuckles, faster!' he said, and the chicken screeched off in pursuit. Eighty miles an hour, ninety, a hundred. At a hundred and ten, with an enormous chicken right on its tail, the Rolls-Royce owner conceded victory and pulled into the middle lane. Chuckles and the vicar's car roared past.

Suddenly disaster struck. The harness broke. Chuckles shot off up the M.1 and the engineless car shuddered to a stop. Within seconds a police car screeched up to the old banger.

'What the devil do you think you're doing,' asked one of the policemen, 'stopping in the middle lane of the M.1?'

'I'm sorry,' said the vicar. 'My big hen's gone.'

*"And do I have to keep on holding this?"*

The invention of the motor car is said to have had a momentous effect on the lives of ordinary people. For the first time, everyone could go where they pleased how they pleased. The motor car was the key to independence. That at least was the theory. Not everyone would agree. John Ketas, for example:

**The automobile did not put the adventure of travel within reach of the common man. Instead, it gave him the opportunity to make himself more and more common.**

Others, like J. E. Morpurgo, welcomed the invention:

**God would not have invented the automobile if He had intended me to walk.**

This respect for cars can verge on idolatry. The world seems to be divided into those who worship the machines and those who hate them. Holden Caulfield, the hero of J. D. Salinger's *The Catcher in the Rye* fell into the latter category:

> **Take most people, they're crazy about cars ... and if they get a brand-new car already they start thinking about trading it in for one that's even newer. I don't even like *old* cars. I mean, they don't even interest me, I'd rather have a goddam horse. A horse is at least *human*, for God's sake.**

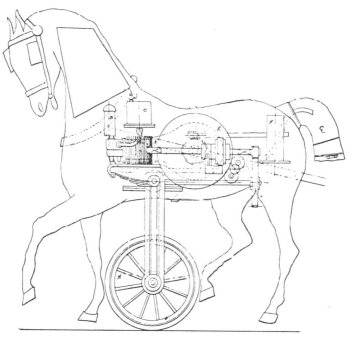

*M. Joseph Mille's petrol tractor.*

But, whatever you think of cars, it's difficult to avoid at least a sneaking respect for the inventors who developed them – and continue to develop them. Every day there's some new improvement available for your car – a new speedometer, an air-cooled gasket leakage condensation inhibitor, an electric butterknife that runs off the battery ... For some people all this electronic sophistication takes the fun away. Here are the views of W. D. H. McCullough and 'Fougasse':

Since the early days of motoring there have been many changes in the apparatus designed to keep drivers posted as to any sensational developments under the bonnet. In the first cars there was little or none of this form of affectation ... Steam coming out of a radiator, or elsewhere, indicated that the water was boiling, and a radiator that slowly became incandescent showed that it had finished doing so. This was all there was to go on ... In those days motorists *were* motorists.

That kind of snobbery still persists. There are still the enthusiasts whose only criterion of worth in a car is age and whose idea of bliss is weekends spent spreadeagled under direct oil drips restoring ancient scrap iron to its original glory. But that is not the only snobbery in the automobile world. Here's another observation from John Ketas:

In the beginning ... a car was a status-symbol, like a boar's tusk in a Papuan's nose.

THE " ALTON " VEIL.

FRONT VIEW.

In Fawn, Grey, Slate and Blue Silk Waterproof. Mica Front, Ventilated.

Each **15/9**

In Gloria ditto .............................each **13/3**

THE "BRAZA" HOOD AND CURTAIN.

In Gloria, various shades ................ **14/0**

The theory is, the more expensive the car, the greater the status of its owner. A report from the *Guardian*:

**Mr Wilfrid Dutton, aged 32, of St. Helens, finds that the acquisition of a 1963 Rolls-Royce Silver Cloud has considerably improved his business – scrap metal. He tours the district in it in search of scrap and no longer finds difficulty in seeing factory directors because he wears overalls. 'Now I merely drive up to the main entrance and, whatever I am wearing, the directors usually come out to see me,' he says.**

Traditionally, advertisers would have us believe, ownership of a Rolls-Royce is the ultimate accolade – for a special type of person. A review from an AA motorists' magazine:

**The boot isn't very big, but a man from the factory warned me about that. He told me: 'A Rolls-Royce owner's luggage, sir, should precede him by rail or air.'**

### WOOLLEN MOTOR CLOTHING

#### (LINED FUR).

Grey Cheviot Cloth Overcoat, lined Hamster, Electric Seal Collar ............from £10 10 0

Grey Cheviot Cloth Overcoat, lined Hamster, Astrachan Collar ....................from 11 5 0

Grey Cheviot Cloth Overcoat, lined Genette, Beaver Collar ....................from 13 10 0

Grey Cheviot Cloth Overcoat, lined Genette, Astrachan Collar ....................from 13 10 0

Grey Cheviot Cloth Overcoat, lined Musquash, Beaver Collar......................from 13 17 6

Grey Cheviot Cloth Overcoat, lined Musquash, Astrachan Collar......................from 13 17 6

And for the ultimate in vehicle snobbery, here's a review from the *Daily Worker*:

> **There are separate air conditioning units for the front and rear compartments. The chauffeur will not have to breathe the same air as the passenger.**

Most would-be car owners start more humbly. It's possible to pick up remarkable bargains by scanning the small ad columns of the newspapers. Here's one from the *Evening Standard*:

> **Ford Prefect 1939 faultless cond. New engine 10,000 miles ago. Available immed. Taxed. Nearest £300 including 6 new-laid eggs for willing buyer.**

And another from the *Cambridge Daily News*:

> **1959 Austin A35, black, heater, new tyres, immaculate, elderly owner exchanged for bath chair.**

Right from the start, cars had sexual overtones. First, there was the status thing, based on the enduring fallacy that possessions make people sexy. But there was more to it than that. Bergen Evans:

> **While the car may limit the size of the family, it is certainly instrumental in getting one started. There is no more irresistable mating call than the imperious horn at the kerb.**

Cars also encourage proximity. A man and a woman alone in a tin box which can be placed anywhere at will is a potentially explosive sexual scenario. There are one or two physical hazards to be overcome, things like gear levers for instance, but these do not deter the avid automobile amorist. Though it's all easier in this country than abroad, according to a Kent paper:

> **And yet in France, the homeland of 'l'amour', many young men must find it less than convenient sitting in a car with their right arm around the girl's waist, having to rely on their left for the appropriate gestures to explain their intentions.**

I daresay they manage. The trouble is that car drivers have been known to assume a sort of *droit de seigneur* with their passengers. A letter published in *Woman's Own*:

> **My friend takes me several rides a week in his employer's car when he has to go into the local town. It worries me, because I know he expects a kiss. I don't mind that, really, but I do feel, as it isn't his car, it is not necessary to kiss him.**

Frequently encounters in cars get even more heated and end up in the courts. Some people will believe anything, according to this legal report from the *Daily Mirror*:

> **Miss Smith had alleged that Jones tried to seduce her in his car, saying that it would make her a better footballer.**

Another from, inevitably, the *News of the World*:

> **Asked by the Judge why she took off her petticoat in B ——'s car on the Saturday, she explained: 'It was rather an expensive one and I knew what he was going to do, but I was so frightened I couldn't stop him. I asked him if I could take it off as I did not want to get it crumpled.'**

Cars are not sexy only because of what happens inside them. The machines themselves seem to have a sexual identity – a feminine one at that. A letter from the *Evening Standard*:

> **I had driven her about 163,000 miles with only two real breakdowns and she was carefully maintained in my own garage. But she has objected violently to her new owner and he has had trouble ever since he took her over. I have always thought that cars have some kind of mechanical soul, and this makes me believe it more than ever.**

'*She keeps making supersonic bangs*'

One interesting by-product of the invention of the motor car has been to put an enormous number of generally law-abiding citizens into conflict with the law. Driving offences can make criminals of us all and the most unexpected people end up in court. A legal report from the *Herts Advertiser*:

> **A St. Albans motorist, summonsed at St. Albans Divisional Sessions on Saturday for a driving offence, was asked by a police inspector: 'After the accident, why did you raise your bowler hat to acknowledge the driver of the other car involved when you did not know him?'**
>
> **The motorist replied: 'The accident had caused the hat to become crammed down over my eyes and ears and – although it might have been polite to raise it to the other driver – I lifted it to alleviate my discomfort.'**

Most motorists who appear in court resent it very much and try to capitalize on their position as much as possible. News from the *Evening Standard*:

> **A man whose car crashed into a telegraph pole agreed at Epsom County Court today that he should pay the**

expense incurred by the Post Office for installing a new post, but claimed that he was entitled to the old one.

'As I am paying for the new post I should at least be allowed to take the old one away,' said Mr William Joseph Mitten, of St. Clair Drive, Worcester Park.

Judge Gordon Clark said: 'You cannot acquire telegraph poles simply by knocking them down.'

The only comfort for convicted motorists is that even the police aren't immune from prosecution. From the *News Chronicle*:

Police Constable Roy Rushmore, booked by a fellow policeman for parking, told Ipswich magistrates yesterday: 'I had to attend this court as a witness. I know that 20 minutes is the parking limit except with special permission from a uniformed policeman. I was in uniform and there was no other policeman about so I gave myself permission.'

Traffic offences become immeasurably more serious when the drivers involved have been drinking. Here's some good advice from Robert Benchley:

One of the measures suggested to aid in the reduction of the number of automobile accidents is the prohibition of gasoline sales to intoxicated drivers. Another good way would be the prohibition of liquor sales to intoxicated drivers.

In spite of the breathalyser, a distressing number of drunken driving cases still end up in court. A report of one from the *Daily Express*:

The other motorist involved declared that Mr H —— smelled of drink. So did a policeman.

And another from the *Bristol Evening Post*:

Dr. Garside said that after the accident Williams did several of the tests quite well. Williams told him he had been to a very good dinner and had a good deal to drink at it. He was certain that his car had touched nothing.

The trouble with cars is that the faster they get, the more dangerous life becomes for everyone. An observation from Lord Dewar:

**There are two classes of pedestrians in these days of reckless motor traffic: the quick and the dead.**

And another from Colin MacInnes:

**Car owners of the world unite: you have nothing to lose but your manners and someone else's life.**

Sometimes injuries from motor cars are not fatal, but they still cause terrible concern among the friends of the victim. Here's a report from an American newspaper:

**It is with real regret that we learn of Mr Wayne's recovery from an automobile accident.**

What a relief it is for us all to know that there are official bodies dedicated to the prevention of accidents. A report from the *Guardian*:

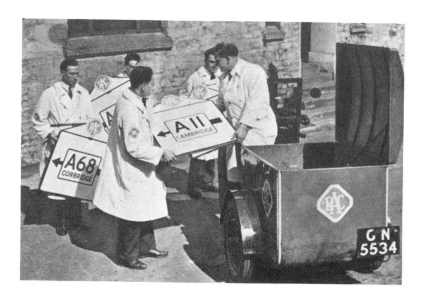

> **Unstone (Derbyshire) Parish Council is seeking the help of Mr Tom Swain, MP, in an attempt to get reversed a decision of the Ministry of Transport that a 100 per cent lighting grant cannot be made for the council's stretch of the A61 'unless there is a considerable increase in the number of serious accidents'.**

One way of keeping down the number of injuries caused by cars is to keep cars off the road. Planners have already worked this one out, according to the *Daily Telegraph*:

> **A maze to muddle motorists is the basis of a plan drawn up by Westminster City Council to create in Pimlico an environmental area with traffic kept to a minimum. It is hoped that through-motorists will be so perplexed they will not enter the area again.**

And that's it for the motor car except for a couple more thoughts. First, for those of mechanical bent, evidence from a defendant in a court in Malling, Kent, quoted in the *Evening Standard*:

**When I tightened the wheel nuts before, I tightened them too tight, so when I went to tighten them again I thought if I didn't tighten them so tight they wouldn't be too tight, but I must have tightened them too loose.**

And finally, a tragic headline from a New Jersey paper:

**Newark Man Gets Broken Nose in Rear End Crash.**

# AIR TRAVEL

Do you know how to recognize Irishmen at airports?
   No, how do you recognize Irishmen at airports?
They are the ones who throw bread to the helicopters.


Two girls meet back at work after their holidays.
   One says to the other, 'You look very brown. Where did you go?'
   'I don't know,' says the other. 'We went by plane '


You know, there are lots of problems with supersonic air flight they haven't really ironed out yet. I mean, when you are going faster than sound, you can't hear what anyone says to you until you catch up with the words. I mean, there was a case on Concorde recently when a bloke said to an air-hostess, 'Could I . . .?' and by the time she'd heard him, he had.


An air-hostess got a job as a bus conductress. Each time the bus moved off she'd say, 'Fasten your safety belts, please.' The day she started seven men got off the bus without their trousers.


TANNOY ANNOUNCEMENT: British Caledonian Flight BR 279 will leave for Delhi at 17.30. Pan American flight for Los Angeles will leave at 17.40. The Aer Lingus flight to Dublin will leave when the little hand is on eight and the big hand is on twelve.


A jet fighter went out of control and the pilot baled out over the Pacific. He lost consciousness and when he came round, he found his head was cradled in the lap of a gorgeous native girl on an exotic island.
   'Oh, you are well,' she murmured with relief. 'What does my brave hero from the silver bird require?'
   'Water,' he said feebly.
   She went into the jungle and brought him back cool spring water in a coconut shell. He drank it gratefully. 'And now what does my brave hero from the silver bird require?'
   'Food,' he whispered.

She soon returned with a roasted boar and fruit and wine. The pilot ate it all and fell into a deep sleep. When he awoke, the girl was still there. 'Now,' she said, 'my brave hero from the silver bird has eaten and rested. Your strength has returned. Would you like to play around?'

'Good heavens,' said the pilot eagerly. 'You mean there's a golf course here as well?'

Air travel is one of the great technological revolutions of the twentieth century. In the words of Saint-Exupery:

**The aeroplane has unveiled for us the true face of the earth.**

But, despite the wonders of the new technology, not everyone welcomed the prospect of man in flight. Henry David Thoreau:

**Thank God, men cannot as yet fly, and lay waste the sky as well as the earth.**

Philip Wylie thought there were other, more pressing priorities:

**We are about to enter the age of flight before we've even developed a chair that a man can sit on comfortably.**

Even though it's now becoming commonplace, air travel remains a profoundly exciting experience. The excitement has been well described by Alexander Chase:

**Lovers of air travel find it exhilarating to hang poised between the illusion of immortality and the fact of death.**

The element of danger is certainly a big part of the thrill. Winston Churchill:

**The air is an extremely dangerous mistress. Once under the spell, most lovers are faithful to the end, which is not always old age.**

Guide to the
Airport of London
(Croydon).

IMPERIAL AIRWAYS

W.H.SCUDDER.

AIR MINISTRY.

PRICE 2d.

The trouble with air travel is that it doesn't only involve sitting in aeroplanes. That's a very small part of the process. Other sorts of travel are involved. Bob Hope:

**I look forward to the day when I can get from Manhattan to Kennedy Airport as quickly as I can get from Kennedy to London.**

Neil McElroy:

**In the space age, man will be able to go around the world in two hours – one hour for flying and the other to get to the airport.**

Al Blake:

**Airplanes aren't really fast and luxurious – it's just that anything would seem fast and luxurious after an hour in an airport bus!**

Air travel is organized and controlled by airlines which, on the whole, are pretty efficient. It can't be an easy job dovetailing all those highly complex schedules and satisfying the booking demands of millions of passengers. Here are a few extracts from letters reputed to have been sent to booking departments of airlines. First, to one in New Jersey:

**Dear Sir, We are four couples planning a joint honeymoon for two weeks. Please send me descriptive literature.**

One from Nebraska:

**Dear Sir, Please can I book two seats on any flight going anywhere that is showing *Gone With the Wind* as an in-flight movie?**

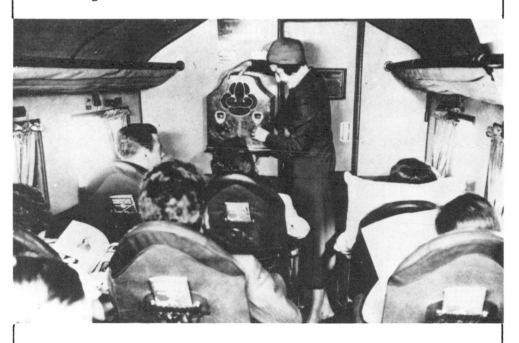

And, nearer home, from Heathrow:

**Dear Sir, I understand that next Monday's flight to Rome is fully booked, but would like a seat with a good view if anyone drops out.**

The airlines, too, sometimes make verbal mistakes, particularly in the way they sell themselves. Good airline slogans stay in the mind, but some of the less effective ones are quickly forgotten. Ones like this:

**Discover the Far East Convenience – fly Cathay Pacific.**

Here's another:

**Come to the fun airline and let us take you for a ride.**

And finally:

**On our airline the planes come first – but the passengers run a close second.**

In spite of the inconveniences of modern air travel, one must not forget the great technological achievement that the aeroplane represents. The desire to be able to fly is as old as mankind. One can trace its development from the legendary Icarus, through Leonardo da Vinci, to the Wright brothers and other pioneers of this century. Not everyone thought it was a good idea. William Law:

**What can you conceive more silly and extravagant than to suppose a man racking his brains, and studying night and day how to fly?**

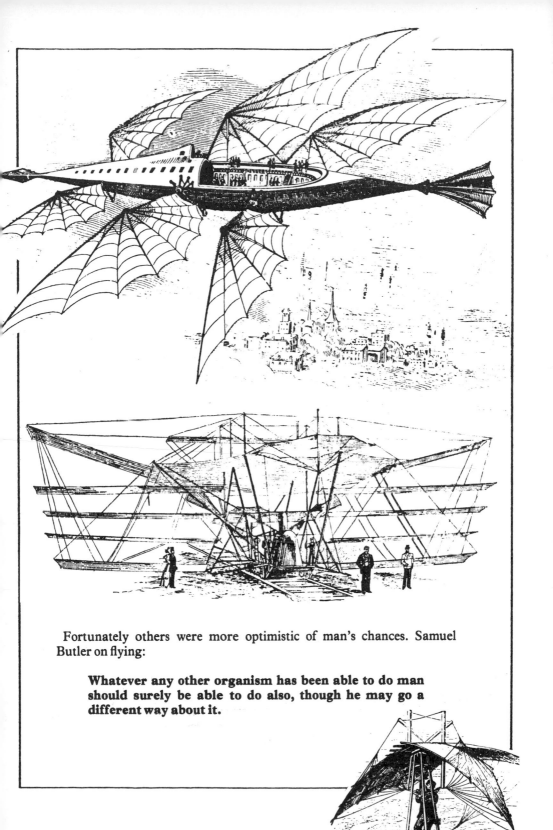

Fortunately others were more optimistic of man's chances. Samuel Butler on flying:

**Whatever any other organism has been able to do man should surely be able to do also, though he may go a different way about it.**

*"You'd think he'd test it himself."*

And man's technological genius did contrive quite a few different ways to go about it. Enormous advances were made, like this one reported in a Sunday newspaper:

> **Thirty thousand feet is a great height for aircraft. Forty thousand feet, to which it is said the Messerschmidt 109F can get, is greater.**

Now the technology is so advanced that space travel is no longer just a science fiction dream. That, like all advances in flying, was frowned on in its infancy. *The Times* printed this note of caution:

> **Let it be said that, even under the best conditions, any trip outside the earth's atmosphere must be reckoned an extremely hazardous undertaking.**

The *Daily Express* was more worried about the moral implications:

> **Russia is planning to send a man and a woman into space together. And they may not be married.**

While the *Glasgow Herald* printed this useful suggestion from a reader:

**In view of the great expense and difficulty involved in firing rockets at the moon, I suggest that future attempts should be made when the moon is full. There would be a better chance of hitting this larger target than hitting the thin crescent present at the time of the latest Russian attempt.**

As space travel has become almost commonplace, so has supersonic travel and it won't be long before there's travel beyond the speed of light.

(There must be a word for it – superluminary travel maybe, or superluminal.) An anonymous limerick:

> There was a young lady named Bright
> Who travelled much faster than light,
>     She started one day
>     In the relative way
> And returned on the previous night.

Apart from the nuisance to the passengers, air travel also creates problems for those of us left on the ground. For a start, there's the problem of privacy. With all kinds of unsuitable people up in the air, isn't there a danger of their prying on the earthbound? Here's a poem by Hilaire Belloc, entitled 'Lord High-Bo':

> Lord High-Bo, getting tired of trains,
> Would binge about in Aero-planes,
> A habit which would not have got
> Him into trouble, had he not
> Neglected what we know to be
> The rule of common courtesy.
> Past bedroom windows he would sail
> And with a most offensive hail
> Disturb the privacy of those
> About to wash or change their clothes.

Another constant complaint of ground-users against air-users is that of noise. There is no way round it – aeroplanes do make a lot of noise, and the faster the plane, the noisier it tends to be. Many of the complaints from the environmental lobby against Concorde are based on noise. But there's always someone ready with a helpful suggestion for problems like sonic-booms. A letter published in the *South Wales Evening Post*:

> A simple solution to this dilemma would be for those who
> live in areas affected by these booms to wear ear muffs.
> The cost of this measure would be trivial compared with
> the profits that we as a nation will make from the sale
> and operation of Concorde. These ear muffs could be
> manufactured in a variety of attractive colours and
> could be issued free under the National Health Service,
> as are spectacles at present.

It's a pity that the worries of the environmentalists are not dealt with like the worries of aeroplane passengers. Inside the plane there is always the establishment figure of the pilot, that avuncular, omniscient presence, who will provide constant reassurance over the tannoy. Helpful messages like this:

> **Ladies and gentlemen, this is your captain speaking. I am delighted to report that we haven't, as we feared, got a bomb on board. At least, if we have, we haven't found it.**

The captain of an aeroplane is the one who's always blamed in the event of disaster and sometimes this is not completely fair. A little verse by Darrel Catling:

> **Don't blame the**
> **pilot**
> **he was**
> **only**
> **semi-pontius**
> **at the time.**

But the captain isn't the only member of staff on a plane. There are also the stewards and, even more important, those repositories of erotic fantasies, the stewardesses, or air-hostesses. Their life is not an easy one. For a start their uniforms keep changing to keep up with passing fashion. A letter from the *Bristol Evening Post*:

> **So the air girls are ordered to shorten their skirts by three inches. Any of them who are not trade unionists may not know that this constitutes an alteration in their conditions of service. Due notice must be given of any such alteration.**

It can't be much fun being constantly at the beck and call not only of fashion but also of a crowd of leering middle-aged executives away from their wives for the first time in years. A sad business. Let's close the chapter with an epitaph on an air-hostess by Simon Brett:

**Here lies a girl whose duties were**
**(Before Death's Pilot summoned her)**
**Sidling up and down the aisle**
**With plastic trays and plastic smile**
**And serving, with each plastic meal,**
**Her plastic-packaged sex appeal.**
**But now her final flight's begun.**
**Her eternal safety belt's undone**
**And, as her drinks were, so is she,**
**Now, forever, duty free.**

# CONSUMER AFFAIRS

"*If you can't do better than that, Riley, you'll find yourself on After Sales Service.*"

Ironmonger, do you have six-inch nails?
    Yes, sir.
Well, scratch my back, will you? It's itching like mad.

'Ere, this broom you sold me's no good. The head's fallen off four times and now the handle's come out.

A man was buying a car on hire purchase and got behind on the repayments. After a time the hire purchase company tried to shame him into paying up and wrote, 'What would your neighbours think if we came and repossessed your car?'
    He wrote back, 'I've taken it up with my neighbours and they all agree it would be a dirty trick.'

Butcher, I don't like all these flies in your shop.
    Well, tell me which ones you don't like, and I'll chase them out for you.

That's a nice suit, Bert. How much did it cost you?
    Two payments and a change of address.

Two Jews who owned a shop were in the pub having a drink.
    'Good heavens!' said one partner suddenly. 'We came away and left the safe open.'
    'What does it matter?' said the other. 'Ain't we both here?'

Chemist, could I have some soap?
    Certainly, sir. Would you like it scented or unscented?
If it's all the same to you, I'll take it with me.

'Ere, shopkeeper, these mothballs you sold me are no good.
    Why not?
I haven't hit a single moth with them.

Ironmonger, could I have a mousetrap, please? And quickly. I've got to catch a bus.
    I'm sorry, we don't sell mousetraps that big.

There's a man on the phone selling clothes props.
  Ask him to hold the line.

'Consumer affairs' is one of those modern sciences which has sprung up recently fully fledged with its own daunting battery of jargon. It was always there; it's just we didn't know what to call it until the expression 'consumer affairs' was invented.

Buying and selling is basic to any form of society and maybe it's even more important in this country than elsewhere. In the famous words of Napoleon:

**England is a nation of shopkeepers.**

If that were true, who would actually do the shopping? Robert Louis Stevenson summed up the basis of economy:

**Everyone lives by selling something.**

But as long as things have been sold there has been suspicion of the sellers by the buyers. Here's a definition from Anarchis, a Scythian philosopher who lived about 600 B.C:

**The market is a place set apart where men may deceive each other.**

Like many things in this country, consumer affairs are surrounded by snobbery. There are still views on where is the right place to shop, even in these times of shrinking spending power. Some people would not be seen dead in a supermarket. And others take the snobbery even further. A report from the *Evening Standard*:

**The landlord, asked at St. Marylebone rent tribunal today why he thought a surgeon, Mr R ——, was an undesirable tenant for a room in Upper Berkeley Street, replied, 'He does his own shopping . . . It is detrimental for this class of house for people to carry shopping. It is not liked by other tenants.'**

Methods of shopping vary in different classes and, as a result, during the last war, rationing affected shoppers in different ways. Here's Lord Woolton, reported in a wartime *Manchester Guardian*:

> **I found that better-off people had many more difficulties than working-class women. They told me how difficult it was not to be able to 'phone and get what they wanted'.**

War's pretty tough. As well as having different methods of shopping and going to different shops, the upper classes also choose their purchases in an idiosyncratic way, according to this cutting from *Men's Wear* magazine:

> **The outfitter in question has one client, a peer's son, who takes his two servants with him when attending for a breeches fitting. If the servants can pull the breeches off his legs he insists on an alteration.**

Consumer affairs are two-sided and so far we have only spoken of the customers. The other side of the counter is just as important. Samuel Butler:

> **Any fool can paint a picture, but it takes a wise man to be able to sell it.**

Selling is an art and indeed a science. The shopkeeper has always to keep abreast with what the customer wants and take account of all the factors which affect this. A report from the *News Chronicle*:

> **A woman buyer for a leading city fashion house said, 'Nobody knows quite why the Birmingham figure should be so difficult. It may be something to do with new regulations in the factories. Almost all the girls sit down to work nowadays, and that is bound to have awful results in the end.'**

A shopkeeper must understand the psychology of his customers. A thought from Earl Wilson:

> **To sell something, tell a woman it's a bargain; tell a man it's deductible.**

Much of this new science is concerned with getting the customer a Fair Deal. Consumer organizations act as watchdogs and spend much of their time investigating the complaints of ill-used shoppers. Some shops are slightly ambivalent in their attitude to complaints – like the one in which this notice appeared:

> **CUSTOMERS SHOULD NOTE THAT ANY COMPLAINTS OF INCIVILITY ON THE PART OF ANY MEMBER OF OUR STAFF WILL BE SEVERELY DEALT WITH.**

Some complaints reflect principally on the complainer. Here's one voiced in a letter to the *Sunday Express*:

> **A Labour Government gets itself elected with an overwhelming majority.**
> **Despite this Socialist Utopia I still cannot purchase a pair of braces with elastic.**

And here's a different cause for complaint from the *Evening Standard*:

> **In a shoplifting case at Southend today it was said that a woman, after stealing a canvas bag, went to the store manager and said it was not suitable. She asked for a 25s. refund.**

*Shop - lifting!*

Consumer affairs seem to be gaining in importance because the society we live in is increasingly consumer oriented. This is not necessarily a bad thing, according to the economist, J. K. Galbraith:

> **Consumer wants can have bizarre, frivolous or even immoral origins, and an admirable case can still be made for a society that seeks to satisfy them. But the case cannot stand if it is the process of satisfying the wants that creates the wants.**

There are serious moral dangers in a consumer society. Too much reliance on property can be a threat to all the old values – like patriotism. A survey from the *Observer*:

> **We asked an assistant to recommend the best dishwasher that money can buy. She came up with an American model. The best tape-recorder? Japanese. The best tent? French. The best gun?**
>
> **'That,' said the assistant, 'depends on what you want to shoot.'**
>
> **'I want to shoot myself.'**
>
> **'In that case,' replied the assistant, unmoved, 'a Webley and Scott should do the trick.'**
>
> **At least I could die backing Britain.**

It's difficult to duck consumer pressures, because we are surrounded by reminders, in the form of advertisements, of all the things we lack. Advertisements can be very persuasive. Here's one from the *Harwich and Dovercourt Standard*:

> **Ladies, start the New Year well, treat hubby to a tip-cart load of manure.**

From a Liverpool greengrocers:

**Fine William pears. Just like tinned.**

One from the *Sheffield Star*:

**I bought a few of your indigestion tablets last week. Now I feel a new man. (Original may be seen on request.)**

Complaints against people in shops nowadays are not so often on grounds of cheating as on grounds of sheer apathy. An observation from George Mikes:

**All English shop assistants are Miltonists. A Miltonist firmly believes that 'they also serve who only stand and wait'.**

But shop assistants can sometimes be very helpful in explaining to customers how the consumer society works. A letter published in *Competitors' Journal*:

**I went into a big store in town and asked the assistant for a small packet of washing powder. She handed me a packet marked Large.**
 **'I'm afraid you didn't understand,' I said, 'I asked for a small packet.'**
 **'That's right, madam,' said the assistant, 'It comes in three sizes – Large, Giant and Super. I gave you the small size – Large.'**

And shop assistants can tell you what stock is and is not available. A letter from *Woman's Mirror:*

**I went to a large store to buy a Bible my nephew requested for his Christmas present. When I asked to see some Bibles I was told, 'Sorry, madam. All our Bibles have been put away, owing to the Christmas rush.'**

And, finally, from a Canadian newspaper:

**There is no substitute for our coffee so do not try it.**

# THE HOME VAPOR BATH AND DISINFECTOR COMPANY,
## 12 East 23d Street, Madison Square, New York.

The following testimonials to the efficiency of the Home Vapor Bath will sustain what is claimed for it, that it is an important hygienic and sanitary improvement, ever ready to render valuable assistance in case of disease, and a luxurious comfort in one's own home. The apparatus, simple in all its appurtenances and in its operation, is made available to all, as it can easily be attached to any bath-tub in any dwelling provided with the ordinary hot-water kitchen boiler, without in any way interfering with the baths hitherto in use in our homes.

72

Very few people, when it comes down to it, like parting with their money and perhaps this is why shopkeepers have always been regarded with such suspicion. Obviously there have always been cheats behind the counter. The double-crossing shopkeeper is a traditional figure. Let's hear some tradesmen's epitaphs:

> **Here lies an ironmonger.**
> **Here his life does stop.**
> **But he won't be long in his coffin,**
> **If the nails were bought in his shop.**

And now a grocer:

> **Here lies a grocer, name of John –**
> **And here it gives me pleasure**
> **To end my epitaph and, like John,**
> **Content you with half measure.**

A butcher:

> **A butcher, name of Tam McNab**
> **Is dead, but not forgotten.**
> **He lies, for once, beneath his slab**
> **And, like his meat, he's rotten.**

And, on the subject of shopping, here's a thought from the American, Ray Fine:

> **What this country needs is a supermarket cart with four**
> **wheels that point in the same direction.**

And finally, let us end the chapter on a note of hope, the hope that we can all follow the proud example of the P. G. Wodehouse character who said:

> **I don't owe a penny to a single soul – not counting**
> **tradesmen, of course.**

# POSTS AND TELEPHONES

The phone rang. The new Irish maid picked it up, muttered a few words into it and slammed it down.

'Who was that?' asked her employer. 'I'm expecting a very important call.'

'Oh, it was some mad idiot, Mr O'Hara. He said it was a long distance from Sydney, Australia. I told him we knew that.'

Why did you become a telephone linesman?

My last job was sending me up the pole.

A man was away on a business trip when he received a telegram from a family friend. It read, 'Regret to inform you your mother-in-law has just died. Do you want cremation, burial or embalming?'

He cabled back straight away: 'All three. Take no chances!'

An old Irish lady wrote to her boy in England: 'Dear Mick, I am writing this slowly because I know you can't read very fast. Please let me know if you don't get this letter.'

Hello, is that McPherson, McPherson, McPherson and McPherson, the solicitors.

Yes.

Could I speak to Mr McPherson, please?

No, I'm sorry, he's on holiday.

Oh, Well, could I speak to Mr McPherson please?

I'm sorry, he's with a client.

Oh, Well, could I speak to Mr McPherson then?

Speaking.

An Irishman goes to see his friend in hospital and the man's lying there with bandages round both his ears.

'Ah, Mick,' says the visitor. 'What happened to your ear?'

'Well, Paddy, somebody phoned me up while I was ironing.'

'But, Mick, what about the other ear?'

'Ah. That was when I phoned for the ambulance.'

A man phones up the wholesalers, Cohen and Goldberg.

'Could I speak to Mr Cohen, please?'

'I'm sorry,' says the girl on the switchboard. 'I'm afraid Mr Cohen's out.'

'Then could I speak to Mr Goldberg, please?'

'I'm afraid he's tied up at the moment, sir.'

'OK, I'll ring back later.'

Half an hour later he tries again. 'Could I speak to Mr Goldberg, please?'

'I'm afraid Mr Goldberg is still tied up, sir.'

'I'll phone back.'

Ten minutes later. 'Mr Goldberg, please.'

'I'm terribly sorry, sir. I'm afraid he's still tied up.'

'Oh, now come on, this is ridiculous. You can't run a business like this – one partner out all day and the other tied up for hours on end. What the hell's going on?'

'I'm sorry, sir. It's just that whenever Mr Cohen goes out he ties up Mr Goldberg.'

The postal and telephone services both perform the valuable function of bringing people together, but like so many worthy institutions, they are often the butts of humour. Sometimes the humour is aimed at genuine inefficiencies in the system, often it derives just from the character of its users. Some people are less keen than others on being brought together. Henry David Thoreau:

> **For my part, I could easily do without the Post Office . . .**
> **I never received more than one or two letters in my life**
> **that were worth the postage.**

The bearers of bad news have always been unpopular. In classical times they tended to be executed. The postman is still held responsible for what he delivers. Douglas Jerrold:

> **A strange volume of real life in the daily packet of the**
> **postman. Eternal love and instant payment.**

The poet William Cowper drew attention to the postman's lack of involvement in his burden:

> **He whistles as he goes, light-hearted wretch,**
> **Cold and yet cheerful; messenger of grief**
> **Perhaps to thousands, and of joy to some.**

All very unfair to the poor postman. Let's return to a time when their work was appreciated. The historian, Herodotus, wrote in their praise in the fifth century B.C:

> **Neither snow, nor rain, nor heat, nor gloom of night**
> **stays these couriers from the swift completion of their**
> **appointed rounds.**

The most common source of anti-G.P.O. humour is the time it takes letters to reach their destinations. Here's a letter sent to *The Times* in 1970 by the Dean of Canterbury:

> **Sir – A few days ago I received a communication addressed to T. A. Becket, Esq., care of the Dean of Canterbury. This must surely be a record in postal delays.**

But this kind of cavilling ignores the many advantages of the British postal system. Here's an unexpected one discovered during the last war and reported in the *Daily Telegraph*:

> **After waiting six days for a passenger boat, Major L. Palmer travelled from Guernsey to Jersey in a Channel mail steamer as a parcel, bearing a label marked O.H.M.S. and accompanied by a postman.**

And, of course, postmen have to put up with the supposed humour of the public. From the *Daily Express*:

A joker in Kentucky mailed packages of transistor radios with the volume turned on full blast. Postmen have already delivered seven packages, all properly stamped and addressed, with musical accompaniment.

And yet, in spite of these abuses, the G.P.O. is still ready to help the humblest correspondent, even when it's a child. A report from the *News Chronicle*:

The Post Office Foreign Mails Section announced that if a child puts a proper stamp on a letter to S. Claus in Greenland, Iceland, Denmark, Switzerland, Finland, or any other foreign country, 'it is forwarded to that country'. The spokesman added, 'Of course, we know that Santa Claus doesn't live in those places. What happens when they reach the various countries we don't know.'

Enough of the post; on to the telephone. Let's start with a definition from Ambrose Bierce:

Telephone: an invention of the devil which abrogates some of the advantages of making a disagreeable person keep his distance.

Here's Ogden Nash on the subject:

Someone invented the telephone,
And interrupted a nation's slumbers,
Ringing wrong but similar numbers.

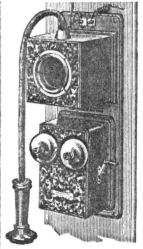
At first the telephone was a rather daunting piece of apparatus which not everyone understood. A piece from the *Oxford Mail*:

> **Urging that workers in remote rural areas should be taught how to use the telephone, Mr Jack Shingfield, a member of the Essex Agricultural Executive Committee, said that recently when a straw stack caught alight at a Little Clacton farm the men called the fire brigade by telegram. The firemen arrived too late.**

The telephone has had a profound sociological effect, but it has also had an effect on the environment, lacing the countryside with wires and spotting city centres with vandalized phone booths. No one seems to realize what phone booths are for. A report from the *Sunday Dispatch*:

> **It was stated that the three men were playing pitch and toss in the street when the street lamps were switched off at 11.40 p.m. To enable them to carry on the game they went to a telephone box, took the directory, and set fire to the pages.**

Telegraph poles have always been a problem and the cause of many environmentalist squabbles. An account of one such from *The Times*:

**Durham Rural District Council's housing committee has decided that five telephones in houses on a council estate at Witton Gilbert must be removed because the poles are an eyesore. Councillor H. Cooper, a member of the housing committee who lives on the council estate but has no home telephone said, 'Unfortunately, we cannot do anything about the poles which spoil the appearance of the estate but we can have the telephones removed.'**

Sometimes one is tempted to wonder what happens to the people who take the major decisions in matters relating to the telephone. Fortunately, the answer is provided in a Freudian misprint from the *Boston Traveler*:

**When telepone directors become obsolete they are sold to waste-paper companies for conversion into pulp. They are torn in two lengthwise, then chopped into small bits in a powerful machine.**

Telephone technique is now part of the essential qualifications for a successful executive. There are all kinds of nuances in how the instrument is used, who speaks to whom first, whether a call is put through by by a secretary, whether the would-be executive is trapped into speaking to a secretary, whether or not he is kept waiting. The telephone can be a very humiliating device. Troy Gordon:

**I don't mind being put on 'hold', but I think they've got me on 'ignore'.**

On the other hand, the telephone can give an immense sense of power. Robert Benchley:

**There is something about saying 'OK' and hanging up the receiver with a bang that kids a man into feeling that he has just pulled off a big deal, even if he has only called up to find out the correct time.**

The trouble is that, however impressive you want to be on the phone, you are at the mercy of the machine. A wrong number, an unobtainable tone, a crossed line, they can all ruin your panache. And if you're dealing through the operator, then you're really putting your dignity on the line. The operators hold all the cards. Here's how Marcel Proust described them:

**The ever infuriated servants of the Mystery, the umbrageous priestesses of the Invisible, the Young Ladies of the Telephone.**

*Telephone Exchange*

While we're on the subject, here's an epitaph on a telephone girl by Simon Brett:

Her friendly 'Number, please' is silent now and gone;
The operator has at last been operated on;
She's been cut off and when you ring, no matter how
     you try,
You'll find she's ex-directory and there'll be no reply.

As well as the normal service of two-way communication, the telephone has also been adapted to give special services – like accurate time checks, test scores, recipes, pop records and so on. Perhaps the most valuable of these special numbers is 999, that great protector of the life and property of the individual. A news story from the *North-Eastern Evening Gazette*:

> **When the accused was fined five shillings at Tower Bridge Court, London, today for being drunk, it was stated that he went into a telephone box, dialled 999, reported that he was very drunk, and asked to be collected.**

The service is there for the police just as much as the general public. Here's a law court report from the *West London Chronicle*:

> **A police sergeant agreed, amid laughter, at West London on Monday that, when he experienced difficulty in dialling 999 to summon assistance, one of two men whom he had arrested loaned him 2d. to make the telephone call.**

Some believe that the telephone is not a medium for conversation at all and should only be used for the tersest of arrangement-making. Somerset Maugham would have agreed with them:

> **In heaven when the blessed use the telephone they will say what they have to say and not a word besides.**

He also made this observation on the uses of the instrument:

> **Some women can't see a telephone without taking the receiver off.**

Taking the receiver off is easy for those of us familiar with the telephone, but every day someone who's never seen one before must, one assumes, make his first stumbling attempts to understand the mystery.

It's presumably for them that all those dialling instructions appear at the beginning of telephone directories. Do you remember that lovely instruction they used to have – 'When dialling an all-figure number be sure to dial all the figures'? Here's an extract from what are supposed to be Japanese dialling instructions, translated into English for the benefit of tourists.

> **Employing the right finger next-door thumb, go in small holes on clock. Numbers in holes correspond to numbers of number. Move clock with finger to make it retire. When it comes back, make go another number. Very impotent – do not make go with new number until clock has gone to bed. Otherwise you will be conjoined with an unsuitable partner.**
>
> **When you have achieved your end, get your finger out.**

Let's conclude with a little poem by Eleanor Bron, entitled *No Answer*.

**I waited**
**For the phone**
**To ring**
**And when at last**
**It didn't**
**I knew it was you.**

# INVENTIONS

A wonderful invention, the X-ray. Once a doctor was demonstrating an X-ray machine to a group of students. There was a patient behind the screen and the doctor said, 'Right, now we can see from the bone structure that the patient's right leg is shorter than his left, which accounts for his limp. You in the front — what would you do in a case like this?'

The student said, 'Oh, I think I should probably limp, too.'

Two cavemen inventors were talking to each other. One said, 'Why don't you invent the wheel?'

His friend said, 'I would, but, if I did, my son'd keep wanting to borrow the car.'

What do you get if you cross a dog with a giraffe?
Something that barks at aeroplanes.

What do you get if you cross a cow with an Arab?
A milk sheikh.

What do you get if you cross a cowboy with a dentist?
Hopalong Cavity.

What do you get if you cross a tambourine with a submarine?
The Salvation Navy.

What do you get if you cross a mouse with an elephant?
Enormous great holes in the skirting board.

What do you get if you cross the Atlantic with the Titanic?
Half way.

Two little boys were paddling in the sea.
'Coo. Aren't your feet dirty?' said one.
'Well, you see,' said the other, 'we didn't have a holiday last year.'

Did you hear about the Irishman who applied for planning permission to move his house four feet so that he could take up the slack on his washing line?

Mummy, Mummy, can I go into the sea for a swim?
   No, dear, the sea's too dirty and polluted.
But Daddy's swimming.
   Well, he's insured.

Inventions have probably brought benefits and miseries to mankind in equal amounts. Certainly there is something magnificent about the creative abilities of the human mind, but unfortunately these abilities are not always directed to the common good. When they are, the benefits are enormous. Francis Bacon:

**The real and legitimate goal of the sciences is the endowment of human life with new inventions and riches.**

There don't seem to be any hard and fast rules about inventions and how and when they occur. Jonathan Swift:

**The greatest inventions were produced in times of ignorance, as the use of the compass, gunpowder and printing; and by the dullest nation, as the Germans.**

Mark Twain:

**Name the greatest of all inventors. Accident.**

But however inventions arise, they cause great excitement when they do. I suppose it's the appeal of novelty. Ralph Waldo Emerson:

**If a man can write a better book, preach a better sermon, or make a better mouse-trap than his neighbour, though he builds his house in the woods, the world will make a beaten path to his door.**

No invention could happen without the dedicated effort and concentration of an innovator with a vision – an inventor. Let's have a definition from Ambrose Bierce:

**Inventor: a person who makes an ingenious arrangement of wheels, levers and springs, and believes it civilization.**

Inventors do not always get the credit for their pioneering work until it is too late to be of much use to them. Fyodor Dostoyevsky:

**Inventors and men of genius have almost always been regarded as fools at the beginning (and very often at the end) of their careers.**

Not only are they regarded as fools, but often as complete madmen. How readily the words 'mad' and 'inventor' go together – and how vivid the image they present to the mind. S. J. Perelman:

**I guess I'm just an old mad scientist at bottom. Give me an underground laboratory, half a dozen atom-smashers, and a beautiful girl in a diaphanous veil waiting to be turned into a chimpanzee, and I care not who writes the nation's laws.**

The process whereby things get invented is a mixture of research and accident. The inventor may just stumble on a world-shattering innovation while looking for something utterly different — even something trivial. Eric Hoffer:

**We are more ready to try the untried when what we do is inconsequential. Hence the remarkable fact that many inventions had their birth as toys.**

As well as accident, there's guesswork, which is important in all areas of science. A short poem by Hilaire Belloc, *The Microbe*:

**The Microbe is so very small**
**You cannot make him out at all,**
**But many sanguine people hope**
**To see him through a microscope.**
**His jointed tongue that lies beneath**
**A hundred curious rows of teeth;**
**His seven tufted tails with lots**
**Of lovely pink and purple spots,**
**On each of which a pattern stands**
**Composed of forty separate bands;**
**His eyebrows of a tender green;**
**All these have never yet been seen –**
**But Scientists, who ought to know,**
**Assure us that they must be so . . .**
**Oh, let us never, never doubt**
**What nobody is sure about.**

But guesswork alone is not sufficient for the inventor. Alfred North Whitehead:

**'Necessity is the mother of invention' is a silly proverb.**
**'Necessity is the mother of futile dodges' is much nearer**
**to the truth. The basis of the growth of modern invention**
**is science, and science is almost wholly the outgrowth of**
**pleasurable intellectual curiosity.**

And that pleasurable intellectual curiosity leads to research. And more research. And experiment and trial and error. And more errors. Sometimes it must get very depressing and make great demands on the would-be inventor's faith in himself. André Gide:

**One does not discover new lands without consenting to**
**lose sight of the shore for a very long time.**

No, it's very hard work. A report from *Design*:

**A designer or manufacturer who keeps his nose glued to**
**his own grindstone will have some difficulty in keeping**
**his ear to the ground at the same time.**

A l'École.

Chantier de Construction electrique.

Un Frotteur électrique

EN L'AN 2000

Le Lawn-Tennis.

EN L'AN 2000

Une Maison roulante de Villégiature.

EN L'AN 2000

Un Hydroplane.

Research sometimes involves experiments on animals – a subject on which people get very heated. I suppose the old argument is true – that anything is justified if the good it does outweighs the harm. With some experiments this justification is difficult to make. From the *Corning Glass Works Magazine*:

> **Recent tests conducted by a zoologist prove that grasshoppers hear with their legs. In all cases the insects hopped when a tuning fork was sounded nearby. There was no reaction to this stimulus, however, when the insects' legs had been removed.**

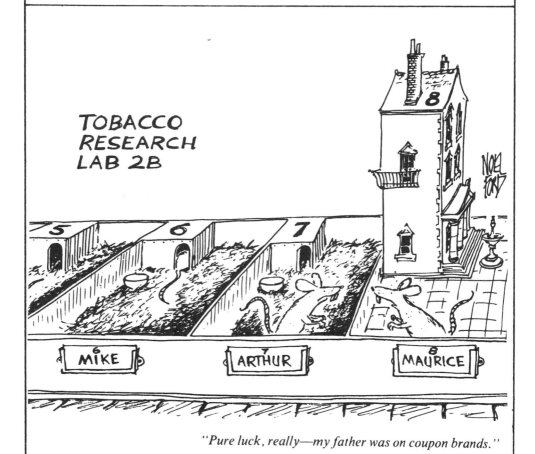

*"Pure luck, really—my father was on coupon brands."*

Mind you, after detailed research you will know all about animals and be able to answer even quite complicated questions about them – unlike the *Detroit News,* in which the following exchange appeared:

**Question: 'How can you tell the age of a snake?'**
**Answer: 'It is extremely difficult to tell the age of a snake**
**unless you know exactly when it was born.'**

A lot of research doesn't happen dramatically in laboratories; it comes from years of painstaking reading. Thank goodness for the library system. From a West Country paper:

**The Librarian reports that we now have in our Reference**
**Library a larger number of boobs than has any other**
**library in the county.**

Mainly, though, it's just trial and error, trial and error. It takes a long time. A Latin proverb:

**Nothing is invented and perfected at the same time.**

All that hard work and experimentation is justified if the end-product is useful. Henry Ward Beecher:

> **A tool is but the extension of a man's hand, and a machine is but a complex tool. And he that invents a machine augments the power of a man and the well-being of mankind.**

And the more you invent, the better you get at it. Ralph Waldo Emerson:

> **Invention breeds invention.**

Alfred North Whitehead:

> **The greatest invention of the nineteenth century was the invention of the method of invention.**

But what of actual inventions? Let's hear of one from that fertile inventor, J. B. Morton, better known as Beachcomber:

> **Dr. Strabismus (whom God preserve) of Utrecht is carrying out research work with a view to crossing salmon with mosquitos. He says it will mean a bite every time for fishermen.**

Unfortunately, many such brilliant inventions never see the light of day. J. K. Galbraith:

> **It is easy to overlook the absence of appreciable advance in an industry. Inventions that are not made, like babies that are not born, are rarely missed.**

In the modern technological age, we've perhaps got rather blasé about inventions. There are so many new developments and they are perfected and marketed so quickly that we tend to take them for granted. Mind you, man can't do everything. Joseph Wood Krutch:

> **Electronic calculators can solve problems which the man who made them cannot solve; but no government-subsidized commission of engineers and physicists could create a worm.**

And not all the side-effects of inventions are desirable. Lewis Mumford:

**By his very success in inventing labour-saving devices, modern man has manufactured an abyss of boredom that only the privileged classes in earlier civilizations have ever fathomed.**

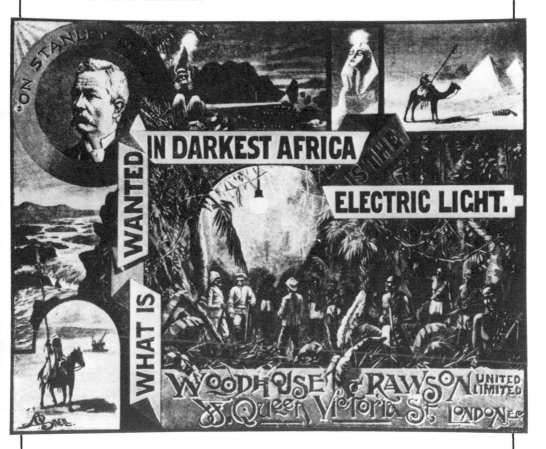

The advances in automation will have their effect on man as a species, according to Frank Lloyd Wright:

**If it keeps up, man will atrophy all his limbs but the push-button finger.**

To conclude the chapter, let's hear the considered opinion of that American falsetto balladeer and philosopher, Tiny Tim:

**Why, the greatest invention in history is the safety pin.**
**The second greatest is perforated toilet paper.**

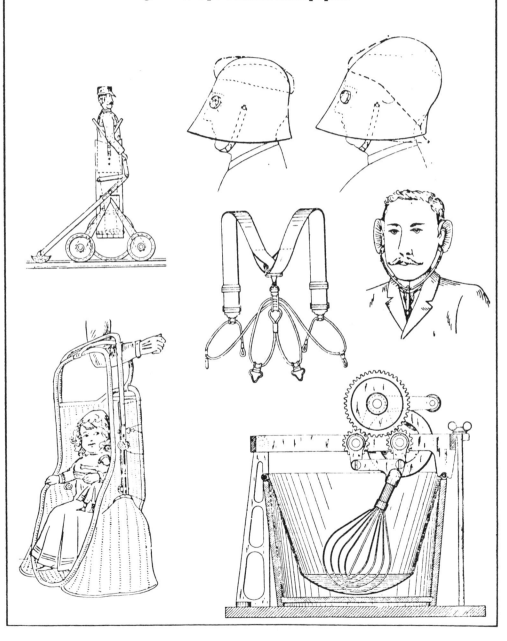

# THE ENVIRONMENT

OVER-POPULATION.

A prim lady saw a young boy in the street with a cigarette hanging out of his mouth.

'Young man, do you know that smoking's a slow poison?'

'That's all right,' he said, 'I'm in no hurry.'


There was an old woman who lived on the Pennines and the rating authorities could never decide whether her home was in Yorkshire or Lancashire. Eventually they sent along an inspector who made the decision that she lived in Yorkshire.

'Ee, thank goodness for that,' she said. 'I've heard the winters are very cold in Lancashire.'


A woman goes to a fortune-teller.

'Tell me,' she says, 'what does it mean if my hand itches?'

'Ah,' said the fortune-teller. 'That means you are going to have visitors.'

'And what does it mean if my head itches?'

'That means they've arrived.'


I had a friend once who lived in a house in a terrible position. There was a tannery to the east of it, a piggery to the west, a glue factory to the north and a refuse dump to the south. Mind you, he always knew which way the wind was blowing.


Waiter, I must complain. The flies are thick in this place.

What do you want – educated ones?


Terrible things, vermin. Do you know, a man booked into a seaside hotel and as he signed the book, a bedbug crawled across the page.

'I'm not staying here,' the man said. 'I've seen bedbugs before, but when they actually come and check which room you're in . . .'

Two Irish builders were working on a house and, because it was in a beauty spot, the walls had to be weatherboarded with cedar planks. They were nailing on the boards and one of them kept sorting through handfuls of nails and throwing a lot of them away.

'What are you doing that for, Mike?' asked his friend.

'Why, Pat, half these nails have got the point on the wrong end.'

'Ah, you eejit!' said Pat. 'Those are for the other side of the house.'

Concern for the environment is currently a popular preoccupation. Such concern has always been subject to the whims of fashion. Decades of apathy are suddenly overtaken by short bursts of enthusiasm for conservation, but then – too quickly – apathy takes over again. I suppose for much of the time people are so absorbed with other matters that they don't have time to notice the world around them. They lose a lot by this. Honoré de Balzac:

**The love of nature is the only love that does not deceive human hopes.**

But men find it easy to forget that fact. Ross Parmenter:

**In remaking the world in the likeness of a steam-heated, air-conditioned metropolis of apartment buildings we have violated one of our essential attributes – our kinship with nature.**

Nowadays, mankind has enormous technical facilities for changing the face of nature. Loudon Wainwright:

**The magnificence of mountains, the serenity of nature – nothing is safe from the idiot marks of man's passing.**

One is more aware of the marks of man's passing in the country than one is in the city. The city has been taken over long ago, but new building and development can still scar virgin country. There has always, from classical times on, been a conflict between the attractions of Town and Country. Dr. Johnson:

**No wise man will go to live in the country, unless he has something to do which can be better done in the country.**

Though in some cases, there's snobbery as a motive, well described by Don Marquis:

> He worked like hell in the country so he could live in the city, where he worked like hell so he could live in the country.

Love and respect for the country are expressed in the work of conservation groups who fight apathy and come up with useful environmental suggestions. From the *Daily Mirror*:

> Why should the ingenious, and often beautiful art of camouflage be confined to the uses of war? A gasworks need be no less efficient because it has the appearance from a distance of a beautiful forest.

Love of the countryside can also be expressed in the care of gardens, though this, surprisingly, sometimes has political overtones. A report from the *Warrington Guardian*:

**Mr John Dewes, Conservative Chairman of Runcorn Division told the Young Conservatives on Monday: 'If a man has a tidy front garden, nine times out of ten he is a Conservative.'**

*"When you sold me that weed-killer you mentioned nothing about possible side-effects!"*

Conservation groups, too, sometimes have political axes to grind — certainly in the view of the American, John N. Mitchell:

**The conservation movement is a breeding ground of Communists and other subversives. We intend to clean them out, even if it means rounding up every bird-watcher in the country.**

Some observers just seem to be impervious to the charms of nature. Another sensitive American, Ronald Reagan:

> **If you've seen one redwood you've seen them all.**

And a report from *The Motor*:

> **If a driver chooses to spoil performance statistics by gazing at scenery, that is his own concern, but this does not affect time/distance relationship which is possible to one who regards natural scenery as an unnecessary excrescence.**

Perhaps the biggest challenge to our environment is man's developing technological ability. New ideas need resources and space — and do not necessarily improve the quality of life. J. B. Priestley:

We cannot get grace from gadgets. In the bakelite house of the future, the dishes may not break, but the heart can. Even a man with ten shower baths may find life stale, flat and unprofitable.

But for others there are other priorities. Let us hear the views of Harley G. Waller, the President of the National Refractory and Brake Company:

If all these nature kooks had their way, America would still be a wilderness from coast to coast. Thank God there are at least a few businessmen who care about the Gross National Product.

Fortunately, in most countries there are strict controls on industrial development and all forms of building. They're not always foolproof, though. From the *News Chronicle*:

Having been refused permission to build a house, the man applied for a licence to build a farm building. This was granted. He then applied ... for permission to convert the building into a dwelling-house. Yesterday this was approved.

And while we're in the area of planning permission, an anonymous limerick:

There was a young lady from Wantage
Of whom the town clerk took advantage.
  Said the borough surveyor,
   'Indeed you must pay 'er.
You've totally altered her frontage.'

THE BRITISH CHARACTER.
DETERMINATION NOT TO PRESERVE THE RURAL AMENITIES.

*"Could you knock up a wing? Mother's coming to stay."*

Man's record in his treatment of the countryside is not very impressive. Jean-Jacques Rousseau:

> **Everything is perfect coming from the hands of the Creator; everything degenerates in the hands of man.**

Some environmental crimes are just carelessness. If only people could be tidy. From the *Bradford Telegraph*:

> **Ilkley is having one of the most successful Bank Holidays for years. Crowds have left a trail of litter on the riverside and moors.**

*"Let's enjoy it while we can—this is where they're going to build the new Leisure Centre."*

And an environmentally – and politically – explosive suggestion from a letter to the *Liverpool Echo*:

> **Citizens should not be expected to place litter in receptacles while there are unemployed who would be willing to sweep litter from the streets.**

*Winter bathing in the Serpentine.*

*Summer bathing in the Serpentine.*

It's not just the ground that gets polluted, there's the air too. This has been the case for a long time, if we are to believe this quotation from Shakespeare's *Julius Caesar*:

**I durst not laugh, for fear of opening my lips and receiving the bad air.**

And, more recently, a quote from Bob Sylvester:

**I asked a coughing friend of mine why he doesn't stop smoking. 'In this town it wouldn't do any good,' he explained. 'I happen to be a chain breather.'**

Then there's the water, a lot of which is horribly polluted. Though that's getting better, if we are to believe this little thought from Geoffrey Bourne:

**Rivers are getting cleaner**
**Happy dace are here again.**

The threat to our water is very serious — not only to our drinking water, but to our seas. Some of the trouble is environmental pollution, some political. A top-secret report from the *Teignmouth Post*:

**The fishery officer reported that Devon's coastal waters had been experiencing the greatest invasion of octopuses for at least fifty years. It was passed on to him by a fisherman in a small Devon port that the reason for the invasion was that Russian trawlers which visited the area some time ago were fitted with tanks containing octopuses, and these were released in the Channel near the coast.**

And could the Russians also be behind this sinister West Country incident, chronicled in the *Daily Herald*?

**About to christen a girl, the Reverend R. G. Crookshank, rector of Bere Ferrers, South Devon, found tadpoles in the font. Now he is leading villagers in demanding a better water supply.**

Everywhere we seem to be beleaguered with threats of pollution. A report on vermin from the *Ipswich Evening Star*:

**Mr C. J. Clarke** spoke of 'thousands of rats' at Blythburgh which, he said, could be seen sitting on the kerbs and laughing at people. They . . . now had taken a dislike to the village constable and were eating their way through the back door.

News of the threats from chemical waste in the *Widnes Weekly News*:

**I think we are stifling initiative here, said Councillor R. Illidge**, criticizing the action of the Highways Committee at the Widnes Town Council meeting on Tuesday night, in refusing an application from a local firm to pump waste acid over a public footpath.

And if you miss these disasters there's always the cheering prospect that another supertanker will run aground and bathe our shores with oil. Do you remember the *Torrey Canyon*? A letter to the *Daily Telegraph*:

**Sir – My brother and his wife have just returned from a holiday in Guernsey. There the bit of oil left from the *Torrey Canyon* is a tourist attraction. People go to see it, peer at it, poke it and spoon it into plastic bags to take home as souvenirs. It makes their holiday. If people don't go quickly there will be none left to see.**

But oil won't be there for ever, either as a tourist attraction or a fuel. Norbert Wiener:

**The more we get out of the world the less we leave, and in the long run we shall have to pay our debts at a time that may be very inconvenient for our own survival.**

It can get very depressing if you think too much about pollution. You can even get suicidal. An item from the *Eastbourne Herald*:

**The Town Clerk reported to the Downs Preservation Committee on an interview with the Reverend R. Q. Nelson regarding his suggestion that notices should be erected on Beachy Head designed to dissuade from suicide persons who might be contemplating it.**

**The Committee recommended that the Town Clerk obtain specialist advice as to whether such notices are likely to achieve their object.**

Interesting that it was the Downs Preservation Committee. Of course, we have a duty to preserve our environment: keep it unsullied, unpolluted, see that it doesn't get spoiled by chemicals or burned. Thank goodness that at least we have an organization to control fire. A report from the *Kentish Times*:

> **The fact that West Wickham fire station is situated in a road which is blocked at both ends was mentioned by Mr F. A. Ruler, Secretary of Hayes Village, on Thursday last week.**

Let's just have one more thought on the environment before the end of the chapter. This one's from *Playboy*:

> **The giant chicken-eating frog will soon be extinct unless we take action now! . . . So for God's sake let's not do anything.**

London going out of Town — or — The March of Bricks & mortar

# THE ARMY

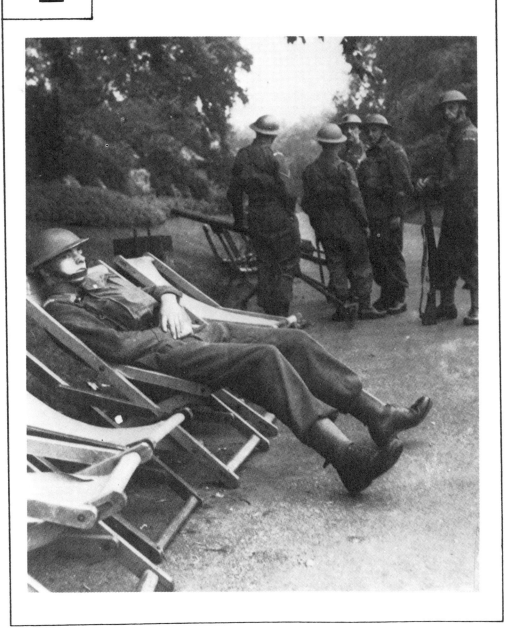

They were doing medical examinations for army entry and a bloke came in with one leg nine inches shorter than the other.

The M.O. said, 'Yes, fine, you're in.'

'Wait a minute,' said the man, 'I've got one leg nine inches shorter than the other.'

'Don't worry,' said the M.O. 'Where you're going, the ground won't be level.'

Another bloke went to the M.O. and when they looked into his ear they found they could see right through and out the other side. They made him a lieutenant.

In my regiment we used to shoot first and ask questions after. Of course, we never got many answers.

OFFICER: Now come on, you. This won't do. You're meant to be firing this rifle at the target and none of your shots are hitting it. Have you any idea where they are going?

RECRUIT: No, sir. All I know is they're leaving this end all right.

An officer was walking across the parade ground when he saw a cigarette stub on the floor with a private standing nearby.

'You, soldier,' he bellowed, 'is that yours?'

'No, it's all right, sir,' said the private, 'you have it – you saw it first.'

And what's wrong with you, Private Jones?

I have a pain in my abdomen, sir.

Listen, soldier – officers have abdomens, NCOs have stomachs. What you've got is a pain in your belly.

An Irish regiment in desperate straits during a battle –

'Sir, sir,' says a private to the commanding officer, 'we're out of ammunition.'

'Well, don't let the enemy know,' said the C.O. 'Whatever you do, keep firing.'

Halt, who goes there?

    Orderly Officer.

Halt, who goes there?

    I've just told you. Orderly Officer.

Halt, who goes there?

    What's the matter with you soldier? Are you deaf or are you being deliberately insolent?

I'm sorry, sir. The sergeant said that if anyone I didn't recognize approached me, I was to shout 'Halt, who goes there?' three times, and then fire.

You know, the Royal Corps of Signals are conducting experiments in crossing a carrier-pigeon with a woodpecker. They want to get a bird that'll knock on the door before delivering its message.

You, soldier, are you happy in the army?

    As happy as can be expected I suppose, sir.

And what were you before you were called up?

    A lot happier.

A young lieutenant was trying to make a phone-call from a phone-box, but he hadn't got the right change, so he stopped a private who was walking by.

    'Have you got some two ps for a tenpence?' he asked.

    'Hang on a sec. I'll have a shufti,' said the soldier.

    'Don't you know the correct way to address an officer?' barked the lieutenant. 'I'll ask you again – have you got some two ps for a tenpence?'

    'No, sir,' said the private.

The army suffers from the fact that it only shows its best in time of war, and war is currently rather unfashionable. As a result, the army is the frequent butt of humour. Without war, military activities, like many others, can look pretty silly. John Fowles:

**Men love war because it allows them to look serious. Because it is the one thing that stops women laughing at them.**

Unfortunately, there is a strong love of war inherent in human nature. Partly, it's the excitement. Dean Inge:

**Hatred and the feeling of solidarity pay a high psychological dividend. The statistics of suicide show that, for non-combatants at least, life is more interesting in war than in peace.**

Also, things get done in wartime. Here's the view of a character in Berthold Brecht's *Mother Courage*:

**What they could do with round here is a good war. What else can you expect with peace running wild all over the place? You know what the trouble with peace is? No organization.**

And war always is supposed to bring political benefits. A definition from Ambrose Bierce:

**Battle: a method of untying with the teeth a political knot that would not yield to the tongue.**

War is a disaster for almost everyone, as Winston Churchill observed:

**War is little more than a catalogue of mistakes and misfortunes.**

Soldiers are the mainstay of wars – indeed without them wars couldn't happen – but the planning is done by generals and the credit, if there is any flying about, tends to go to generals, too. This is not a new state of affairs. Here's a quotation from *Andromaque* by Euripides:

**When the public sets a war memorial up, do those who really sweated get the credit? Oh no! Some general wangles the prestige.**

In war the soldier is the last person to be considered and certainly wars don't start with soldiers. Will Rogers:

**Diplomats are just as essential to starting a war as soldiers are for finishing it. You take diplomacy out of war and the thing would fall flat in a week.**

Soldiers don't always have total faith in their leaders. Aubrey Menen:

**It is the man who is afraid of the *enemy's* General Staff that is a coward; the man who is afraid of his own is merely an old soldier.**

War has changed in the last century, and now it doesn't only involve soldiers. J. K. Galbraith:

**One of the tolerable features of old-fashioned wars was that the military planner could proceed with his task in the reasonably secure knowledge that in the event of hostilities, someone else would be killed.**

One quality which is traditionally assumed in army personnel, whether generals or privates, is lack of imagination. Or, in jokes, stupidity. Here's a telling headline from a wartime *Daily Herald*:

**War Office Admits Officers Need Intelligence.**

TOMMY IN PEACE AND TOMMY IN WAR

Part of the reason why the army has an image of thickness is that army discipline demands instant obedience to orders, often at the expense of thought. H. G. Wells:

> **The army ages men sooner than the law and philosophy; it exposes them more freely to germs, which undermine and destroy, and it shelters them more completely from thought, which stimulates and preserves.**

Gottfried Reinhart:

> **You know, there are three kinds of intelligence – the intelligence of man, the intelligence of the animal, and the intelligence of the military. In that order.**

Joseph Joubert:

> **The sound of the drum drives out thought; for that very reason it is the most military of instruments.**

But one shouldn't be too dismissive of the military intellect. The army has always been very selective in its choice of men. A report from the *News Chronicle*:

> **A man under statutory supervision as a mental defective has joined the forces and been made a corporal, says a report of the special services after-care sub-committee of Birmingham Education Committee.**

The army expects to get a fairly mixed bunch of young men joining its ranks; in fact, it prides itself on knocking the corners off and turning them into soldiers. Perhaps this would be a good moment for another definition from Ambrose Bierce:

**Recruit: a person distinguishable from a civilian by his uniform and from a soldier by his gait.**

Bierce also wrote a little poem about a recruit:

**Fresh from the farm or factory or street,**
**His marching, in pursuit or in retreat,**
**Were an impressive martial spectacle**
**Except for two impediments – his feet.**

But what's it actually like in the army? Though it's a closed society, we can get some inkling from newspaper reports like this one preserved from the *Daily Graphic*:

Ex-soldier, fined £1 at Chatham yesterday for stealing food from Chatham barracks, said he had spent such a long time in the army that it had become a habit.

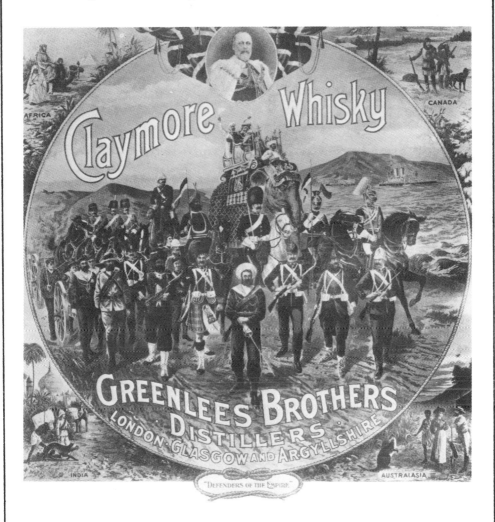

Mind you, such behaviour is, of course, frowned upon in the army. Discipline is very rigid and punishments are severe. Here's an extract from a War Office statement made in the House of Commons:

**Military Prisons. Object 1. The object of penal establishments will be the rehabilitation of the soldier under sentence as a soldier, and to fit him in every way for a return to his unit. In cases where this rehabilitation as a soldier is impossible (due to the incapability of the man himself), the object will be to prepare him for a return to civil life. This latter course will not be adopted except in the most stubborn cases.**

There are many illusions about army life, and one is that war is glamorous. On that subject, here's what Harold W. Ross had to say about Ernest Hemingway's book, *A Farewell to Arms*:

**I understand the hero keeps getting in bed with women, and the war wasn't fought that way.**

No, the way the war was fought, and the way all wars have ever been fought, was by the book. The army is a minefield of regulations – right from the moment you join up. Here's an extract from the application form:

**Proof of birth should be securely pinned between Pages 2
and 3 of this form.**

And the regulations continue at all levels. Especially on matters of
discipline and punishment. An extract from a military guide:

**The more serious of these offences are punishable by
death, and some of them carry heavier penalties when
committed on active service.**

The army has to be tough. Discipline is the basis of efficiency. That's
why soldiers do all that drill. Here's a letter to the *News Chronicle*:

**I was watching a squad of soldiers drilling on the barrack
square and was surprised to see one of them marching
with two rifles (at the short trail). Upon asking the
reason for this, I was informed by a sergeant that the
owner of the second rifle was ill, but his rifle had to go on
parade just the same as usual.**

Care of weapons is very important in the army. After all, weapons are
the basis of military strength. Which reminds me of a famous schoolboy
howler:

**If his rifle fails, the British soldier always has the good
old bayonet to fall back on.**

He probably won't need it, though. The technology of war gets daily
more sophisticated. Will Rogers:

**You can't say civilization don't advance, however, for in
every war they kill you a new way.**

In former centuries the hardware of killing was fairly basic. Let's have
another definition from Ambrose Bierce's *Devil's Dictionary*:

**Gunpowder: an agency employed by civilized nations for
the settlement of disputes which might become
troublesome if left unadjusted.**

Nowadays weapons are more sophisticated. From the *Daily Mail*:

**There is a weapon of the future, too: the air-launched guided missile fitted with a ram-jet engine, cheap to build, fast and devilish in action.**

**Dr. Bush believes it may yet bring a feeling of security to the world.**

And every day a new and more devilish weapon is invented. Here's one devised by Beachcomber's famous character, Dr. Strabismus (whom God preserve) of Utrecht:

**The Doctor is said also to have invented an extraordinary weapon which will make war less brutal. It is described as a very powerful liquid which rots braces at a distance of a mile. This liquid, which is sprayed out of a sprayer, has no ill effect. It smells like a spring morning. But it is deadly to the material from which braces are made. Within an hour of an attack by this liquid – which is heavier than air – the braces begin to rot; and finally disintegrate. The air becomes full of the rustle and plop of falling breeches, and the hapless infantrymen find that their movements are impeded by the descended garments. Also, the idly flapping shirts give them a sense of inferiority.**

But we're in danger of getting too cynical about military affairs. Let us remember the glory and dignity of the army. A letter to the *News Chronicle*:

**As a small child out with my father I was watching a Guardsman on duty. As he passed us I said, in childish innocence, 'You've got a muff on your head.'**

**My father reacted angrily. I got a good whack and he said, 'That is the Queen's uniform. Don't you ever dare say such a thing again.'**

**I never did.**

Perhaps the time when one sees the army at its most impressive is at a big parade, when the splendour and pageantry must stir even the most cynical of spirits. But that sort of event takes a lot of forethought and planning. From the *Daily Express*:

The Coldstream Guards are taking strict precautions to stop men fainting at the Trooping the Colour ceremony on Horse Guards parade, London, next month.

Men below the rank of sergeant are to be confined to barracks, and married men condemned to bachelor barrack beds, on the night before the big parades.

Just a couple of final thoughts on the army. First, a report from *Courier,* the Post Office staff magazine:

> **The BBC gave 17-year-old Martin May £30 for starring in a TV documentary about how good life was in the army. But then Martin shocked the brass-hats by using the money to buy himself out and join the Post Office.**

And, finally, from Oscar Wilde:

> **As long as war is regarded as wicked, it will always have its fascination. When it is looked upon as vulgar, it will cease to be popular.**

There was a galley in the Roman navy full of galley-slaves and one day one of the slaves died at his bench. Immediately all the guards got out their whips and started lashing the rest of the slaves.

'Hey, that's a bit much,' said one of them. 'What've we done? What's all this about?'

'Oh, didn't you know?' said the chief guard. 'When someone goes we always have a whip-round.'

I had a friend who was in the navy during the war. Do you know, he was the first sailor in history to get seasick in the recruiting office.

Ordinary Seaman Smith, you have been found guilty of indiscipline and you are sentenced to seven days on bread and water. How do you like that?

Toasted, sir, if it's all the same to you.

A policeman was on the beat in Portsmouth when he found a sailor lying on the ground with blood all over his face.

He picked the man up and said, 'Could you describe the man who hit you?'

'That's what I was doing when he did hit me,' said the sailor.

As you know, sailors at sea have lots of pin-ups of girls on their walls. They don't use any pins, though – the heavy breathing keeps them up.

The Captain was inspecting the sailor's quarters on a big aircraft carrier.

'Petty Officer,' he bellowed. 'Do you know that there are several articles of women's underwear hanging all over the washroom?'

'Yes, sir,' came the reply. 'It was the married men's idea. They've been at sea so long they're getting homesick.'

Did you hear about the Irishman who hijacked a submarine and asked for a parachute?

The resident bore was pontificating in the Naval Club.

'Oh yes, worst thing that happened to me was during the war in the Pacific. My troopship was torpedoed and I had to live for a fortnight on a tin of beans.'

'Good heavens!' said one of his listeners. 'How on earth did you manage to stay on?'

There was a girl once who wanted to go to America but she couldn't afford the fare, so she went down to the docks, met the captain of a ship and told him her problem. She was a very pretty girl and it didn't take the captain long to come up with a solution.

'Look,' he said, 'all you have to do is to stay in my cabin for the trip and when we get to America, I'll tell you.'

The girl was game, and she stayed in his cabin. She didn't see anyone except the captain until after about a fortnight a steward came into the cabin and asked what she was doing there. The girl burst into tears and told him all about how she wanted to get to America and this was the only way she could do it.

He said, 'Well, you'll be a hell of a time getting there. This is the Isle of Wight ferry!'

The lure of the sea is strong – or so we are told. Certainly for years a large number of British men have gone down to the sea in ships (and a large number have gone down in the sea in ships). It's supposed to be because we are an island people – living on a precious stone set in a silver sea. Certainly from earliest times it was clear to anyone who wanted to get out of England that he would have to cross the water. And that for the defence of our island we would need a navy.

Attitudes to the sea have always varied. Hilaire Belloc was ambivalent on the subject:

> **To sail the sea is an occupation at once repulsive and attractive.**

Joseph Conrad was more mystical about it:

> **The sea never changes and its works, for all the talk of men, are wrapped in mystery.**

But to the real enthusiast, the type who is said to have salt water in his veins, the sea is the first priority of life, overriding everything else. Brooks Atkinson:

> **Land was created to provide a place for steamers to visit.**

The men who are put in charge of the Senior Service are not always the most obvious choices. Here's the view of Sir Edward Carson who got the job in the 1916 coalition:

> **My only qualification for being put in charge of the navy is that I am very much at sea.**

What engaging British honesty! Let's have another example of that quality – a remark attributed to Vice Admiral Beatty at the Battle of Jutland as he watched the sinking of his country's battle-cruisers:

> **There seems to be something wrong with our bloody ships today.**

But the British sailor keeps his cool in moments of victory as well as defeat. Here's a report from *Reynolds News*:

> **'It was a quite thrilling moment when the U-boat sank,'**
> **he said, 'but such is the sang-froid of the modern British**
> **seaman that there was no burst of cheering, only a little**
> **polite hand-clapping from the gun crews.'**

The one thing sailors can't do in a disaster is to comfort themselves that worse things happen at sea. The dangers of naval encounters are enormous. A report from a daily paper:

> **All the six main workships were destroyed, five of them**
> **severely.**

But even without the devastations of warfare, the sea has other hazards to put off all but the most intrepid. Dr. Johnson was not one of the most intrepid:

> **No man will be a sailor who has contrivance enough to**
> **get himself into jail; for being in a ship is being in a jail,**
> **with the chance of being drowned. A man in jail has**
> **more room, more food and commonly better company.**

Douglas Jerrold was also wary:

**Love the sea? I dote upon it – from the beach.**

And many of us who like the idea of boats get less enthusiastic when the seas get choppy. Here's some unhelpful comfort from Jerome K. Jerome:

**It is a curious fact, but nobody is ever seasick – on land.**

However, in a rough sea it doesn't take long for fair-weather sailors to start praying. Samuel Butler:

**How holy people look when they are seasick.**

And yet, in spite of its hazards, the sea still has magnetic powers of attraction. There are some people who just have to be sailors. A description of one such by Spike Milligan:

**He told me he had the sea in his blood and, believe me, you can see where it gets in.**

Sailors are notorious for strange habits, as the Rev. Richard Harris Barham recognized in his poem, *Misadventures at Margate*:

**It's very odd that Sailor-men should talk so very queer.**

And a report from the *Kensington News*:

**When asked by counsel how he knew that they were transvestites he said he had spent $2\frac{1}{2}$ years in the merchant navy and he could recognize them.**

Another thing that sea-faring men are noted for is their love of drink. Here's a clipping from the *News Chronicle*:

**The accused, of no fixed abode, said to have an incurable urge for drinking the liquor out of ships' compasses, was sentenced yesterday at Aberdeen to four months' imprisonment for stealing a gallon of mixture from the compass of a trawler berthed at Aberdeen.**

But, in spite of their little quirks, sailors have to be very heroic. Danger is never far away when you're on the sea and everyone who sails there must be alert at all times. From a Scottish newspaper:

**Mr Campbell, who was on the boat deck jumped to the rails and threw a lifeboat to the drowning man.**

Drowning is the sailor's nightmare (and quite a few other people's nightmare, too). A little Shakespearian verse from June Mercer Langfield:

**Full fathom five thy father lies
His aqualung was the wrong size.**

But don't let's lose sight of the navy as a great military force and the strength of our defences. Let us never forget the names of our great seafarers: Drake, Frobisher, Hawkins, Nelson. Actually, do you remember that lovely *Radio Times* billing there was for Nelson?

**Radio Four – 7.30. The Life of Horatio Nelson (for details see top of column).**

And, in similar vein, let's hear from a book catalogue of a saga of naval heroism:

**'The Teeth of the Storm' – Second Impression – Two Large Plates.**

Gun Drill

Nowadays recruitment into the navy is voluntary, but there was a time when the job was done by force. Those were the days of the press gang. On that subject, here is Thomas Hood's Pathetic Ballad, *Faithless Sally Brown*:

Young Ben he was a nice young man,
    A carpenter by trade;
And he fell in love with Sally Brown,
    That was a lady's maid.

But as they fetch'd a walk one day,
    They met a press-gang crew;
And Sally she did faint away,
    Whilst Ben he was brought to.

The Boatswain swore with wicked words,
    Enough to shock a saint,
That though she did seem in a fit,
    'Twas nothing but a feint.

'Come, girl,' said he, 'hold up your head,
    He'll be as good as me;
For when your swain is in our boat,
    A boatswain he will be.'

So when they'd made their game of her,
    And taken off her elf,
She roused, and found she only was
    A-coming to herself.

'And is he gone, and is he gone?'
    She cried, and wept outright;
'Then I will to the water side,
    And see him out of sight.'

A waterman came up to her,
    'Now, young woman,' said he,
'If you weep on so, you will make
    Eye-water in the sea.'

'Alas! they've taken my beau, Ben,
    To sail with old Benbow.'
And her woe began to run afresh,
    As if she had said Gee woe!

Says he, 'They've only taken him
  To the Tender ship, you see.'
'The Tender-ship!' cried Sally Brown,
  'What a hard-ship that must be!'

Now Ben had sail'd to many a place
  That's underneath the world;
But in two years the ship came home,
  And all the sails were furl'd.

But when he call'd on Sally Brown,
  To see how she went on.
He found she'd got another Ben,
  Whose Christian-name was John.

'Oh Sally Brown, Oh Sally Brown,
  How could you serve me so?
I've met with many a breeze before,
  But never such a blow!'

Then reading on his 'bacco box,
  He heaved a heavy sigh,
And then began to eye his pipe,
  And then to pipe his eye.

And then he tried to sing 'All's Well',
  But could not, though he tried;
His head was turn'd, and so he chew'd
  His pigtail till he died.

His death, which happen'd in his birth,
  At forty-odd befell:
They went and told the sexton, and
  The sexton toll'd the bell.

Like all branches of the forces, the navy is a tangled web of regulations – or at least so it seems to the outsider. However, attempts are being made to clarify the role and activities of the Senior Service. From the *Sevenoaks News*:

> **Royal Navy 'At Home'. Opportunities to tell a captain what to do with his ship will be afforded to members of the public.**

But the reach of the naval authorities is long, as can be demonstrated by this news story from an old *Daily Telegraph*:

> **Newquay Council, wishing to repair some of the boats on their children's boating lake, applied to the Board of Trade for a licence to use 16 cubic feet of timber for the purpose. The Board of Trade has returned their application and told them it should have been sent to the Admiralty.**

In common with the other forces, the navy is very insistent on rank and the respect due to rank. This can be very clearly demonstrated by the following extract from an Admiralty Stores List:

> **Pots, Chamber, plain.**
> **Pots, Chamber, with Admiralty mongram in blue, for hospital use.**
> **Pots, Chamber, fluted, with royal cypher in gold, for Flag Officers only.**
> **Pots, Chamber, round, rubber, lunatic.**

The strength and glory of the navy is, of course, her ships and it is small wonder that a great ceremony is made of the launching of each new vessel. From a provincial newspaper:

> **The vessel left the ways at noon, and safely took the water before her scheduled time. Before leaving the ways Lady White was able to perform the launching ceremony. There was no danger that she would collapse sideways.**

Ships are constantly being improved to attain new feats of efficiency and speed. A report from the *Johannesburg Star*:

# VICTORIA CROSS

## THE

## NEW ORDER OF VALOUR

FOR THE       NAVY.

JOHN SULLIVAN, (BOATSWAIN'S MATE) DELIBERATELY PLACING A FLAG, UNDER A HEAVY FIRE, APRIL 10, 1855.

JOHN BYTHESEA (COMM.) AND W. JOHNSTONE, (STOKER) SEIZING THE RUSSIAN MAIL AND DESPATCHES.

G. B. POWELL, LIEUT. H.M.S. MEEONE UNDER A HEAVY FIRE, THE CREW OF A ROCKET BOAT.

G. F. DAY (COMM.) RECONNOITERING THE ENEMY'S VESSELS IN THE STRAITS OF GENITCHI.

JOSEPH KELLAWAY (BOATSWAIN) MADE PRISONER BY THE RUSSIANS WHILE ATTEMPTING TO SAVE IN Mr. ODEVAINE.

W. N. W. HEWETT (LIEUT) REFUSING TO SPIKE THE GUN IN THE LANCASTER BATTERY.

HONOUR TO THE BRAVE

During the war on several occasions the *Queen Elizabeth* attained a speed of 31 knots and he thought she could possibly exceed this speed if pushed.

In time of peace the navy's job is largely a policing one – seeing that other sea-users obey international laws and keep out of trouble. This work is carried on with the customary unfailing British courtesy. A report from the *Daily Express*:

A spokesman from the Ministry said last night: 'Patrol launches have orders not to order trawlers away from the area. They merely inform the skippers that they are in an area where bombing is about to commence. They usually co-operate by moving.'

And that's about it for the navy. Let's close the chapter with an anonymous epitaph on a sailor.

Here lies a tar who all his life
Did play the Tartar to his wife;
But he was drowned off Zanzibar,
So now it's Tartar tar, ta-ta.

OFFICERS TUBBING. "PUMP AWAY, BOYS"